I Remember

Self Portrait *by Marian Cannon Schlesinger, 1936*

I REMEMBER

A LIFE OF POLITICS, PAINTING AND PEOPLE

Marian Cannon Schlesinger

TIDEPOOL PRESS
Cambridge, Massachusetts

TidePool Press
6 Maple Avenue, Cambridge, Massachusetts 02139
www.tidepoolpress.com

For information, address:
TidePool Press
7 Front Street, Maynard, Massachusetts 01754

Printed in the United States

Library of Congress Cataloging-in-Publication Data

Schlesinger, Marian Cannon, 1912-
    I Remember: A Life of Politics, Painting and People
    p.cm.
    ISBN 0-9755557-8-1/978-0-9755557-8-1
    1. Schlesinger, Marian Cannon 2. Cambridge—United States—
    Biography 3. Memoir 4. Politics I. Title.

    2011939554

For Andy
with much love and appreciation
of his never failing help and advice

BOOKS BY MARIAN CANNON SCHLESINGER

San Bao and His Adventures in Peking (1939)

Children of the Fiery Mountain (1940)

Peter Is Sweeter (1942)

Twins at My House (1945)

The Colonial Williamsburg Coloring Book (1948)

Snatched from Oblivion (1979)

TABLE OF CONTENTS

Introduction

SOME YEARS AGO, I published a book, *Snatched From Oblivion: A Cambridge Memoir*, an account of growing up as an academic child in Cambridge, Massachusetts. At hand were ten volumes of my mother's vivid letters written from Cambridge over the first four decades of the last century to members of her family, her mother in St. Paul, Minnesota, her sisters, her children and various friends and acquaintances. These letters provided a rich vein of information and impressions of a life and a community changed beyond recognition in our contemporary world.

My mother, Cornelia James Cannon, and my father, Dr. Walter Bradford Cannon, both natives of St. Paul, Minnesota, had come east to college, my father graduating from Harvard College in 1896, my mother from Radcliffe College in 1899. My father went on to the Harvard Medical School where, after graduation, he became an instructor in physiology and subsequently the Francis Lee Higginson Professor of Physiology for forty years.

My mother not only brought up five children, but also became a best-selling novelist and a lively community activist. My parents lived their entire adult lives in Cambridge and my mother recorded those years in her letters in evocative detail, prompting in me a flood of memories and making my memoir possible. It became an account of Cambridge characters, local politics, college life, town-and-gown confrontations, and travels in Italy and China in the 1930s, as well as reminiscences of my childhood in an enormous household of high-spirited individuals.

Through all its alterations, Cambridge has consistently been a community hospitable to originals and nonconformists. Above all, it has been a community of remarkable women, from Margaret Fuller to Julia Child. In my small corner of the city, I number among my female neighbors, a theologian, a concert violinist, a Russian translator, a book binder, two art historians, four or five teachers and professors, four or five writers, two psychiatrists, two artists, and a judge.

It goes without saying, among the free-spirited ladies of Cambridge, that through the centuries "doing your own thing" was an established practice long before being raised to a general principle. They looked upon males as frail creatures who had to be handled and propitiated like small children. Having dealt with the men by placing them on pedestals (their accustomed perches where they happily sat), the ladies went ahead with the serious business of their lives, their own self improvement, whether it lay in intellectual pursuits, in social reform, in educational reform, or in the arts or literature. All this I had tried to capture in my book. And so, having gotten the bee in my bonnet with that book, I decided to go on to chronicle the next four or five decades of a long life, recording the rest of the story: my life as a citizen, a traveler, a wife, a mother, a friend, a critic, a writer and an artist.

Horse *by MCS, 2011*

— 1 —

A Cambridge Education

HOUSES SEEM TO HAVE BEEN an important factor in my life, not
only the house in which I live today, where I retreated after my
divorce to figure out what to do with the rest of my life, but
another rambling Cambridge house in which I spent my childhood. Painted a drab gray, the usual color of old Cambridge
houses, it sat in a large yard with a rustic "summer house" in one
corner, a tangle of rose bushes to one side, and a row of bridal
wreath shrubs, snowy white in the spring, in front. Like many
old Cambridge houses, ours has since been moved twice and is
now shorn of its portico and porches where we played hopscotch
and jumped rope. Today it sits on Prescott Street and serves as
the office of the Harvard dean of freshmen.

There was nothing nuclear about our family, consisting of five
children—one boy and four girls—my mother and father, and
my two maiden aunts, both professional women, one, a pioneer in
medical social work, the other, the owner of a charming shop for
children in Harvard Square. Added to the nine was a parade of

I

visiting physiologists, Radcliffe classmates of my mother, homeless students, and hordes of friends of us children. Flanked on one side by the Semitic Museum, on the other by the Harvard University Press, our large Victorian house sat across the street from what was then the Germanic Museum. Up the street were the laboratories and the Agassiz and Peabody museums. We were almost completely surrounded by academic institutions. And so numerous were the children and friends thronging our house that we were thought to be something of an INSTITUTION ourselves. A student meeting one of my aunts reportedly exclaimed, on learning she lived at 2 Divinity Avenue, "But I thought it was an orphan asylum!"

What was Cambridge like when my parents moved here early in the twentieth century and raised five children? It was, in many ways, a divided city, its neighborhoods isolated from one another for all sorts of reasons—historical, economic, and ethnic. There was Old Cambridge, the site of the original settlement and of Harvard College, Yankee to the bone, its citizens living along streets fanning out from present-day Harvard Square toward Brattle Street. And there was the town of town-and-gown, the majority of the city's population, including pockets of old Yankee stock of ancient lineage and neighborhoods of Irish, Italian, and Portuguese immigrants, more recently arrived.

In this sharply divided town, no group was more isolated than the academic community. Though always the pride of Old Cambridge, Harvard College was regarded as an institution apart. The family-oriented society of Brattle Street kept its distance in the presence of "scholarship" and "learning." These

*The Cannon children, (standing) Linda, Bradford
(sitting) Marian, Helen, Wilma, 1920*

endowments were respected as admirable social benefits, but produced in old Cantabridgians feelings of insecurity. A community of intellectuals, especially one increasingly peopled by "men from away," whose names were unfamiliar, did not make for social ease. The rest of Cambridge was a trackless wilderness to both Old Cambridge and the academic community.

We were academic children with a vengeance, surrounded by faceless laboratories and spooky museums. Only over the back fence did the real world begin where people lived in huge houses and had uniformed maids and Irish gardeners, where fathers went to work in Boston and all the children were having their teeth straightened. It seemed to be a no-man's-land of wealth and privilege, as remote from our lives as the corridors of the Semitic Museum. In fact, it was in this part of Cambridge that the psychologist William James, the philosopher Josiah Royce, and other distinguished members of the Harvard faculty lived with their families in comfortable houses on the grounds of what was once the Charles Eliot Norton estate. A scattering of lawyers and judges and a businessman or two lived there, too. But as far as we children were concerned, they were like creatures from another sphere, and we kept our eyes out for their Irish maids when we climbed their fences and sprinted through their gardens on mysterious errands.

Once, when a "college cop" stopped my sister Helen and a "best" friend on their way home from school, cross-country, they expostulated in self-righteous indignation, "Our fathers are Harvard professors, and we can do whatever we want!" This magnificent bit of priggishness was apparently our shield against the world. It would never do today! Nor would a remark, reported by a neighbor, made by another "college cop," a philosophical, red-faced Irishman who kept a solicitous eye out for us children. "It takes these Italians and furriners a long time to learn that Cambridge is not a place but a opportunity."

Cambridge was full of sounds in my childhood. The seven o'clock whistles of the factories in East Cambridge tumbled us out of bed on school days in the dark of winter, and the mournful moan of foghorns from the Mystic River haunted the freezing

4

drizzle of a March afternoon. There was a cacophony of bells and clocks: the old Memorial Hall tower clock booming out the hours, day and night; the metallic striking of the half and quarter hours by the chimes of St. Paul Catholic Church on Bow Street; and distant, unknown bells, telling the hour at odd moments out of phase with other timepieces, or summoning the faithful to Mass or vespers. The tinkle of bells on the harnesses of horses dragging ice pungs is a remote and dreamlike memory, but the lowing of cattle driven through the streets to the abattoir in Brighton, mixed with the shouts and curses of the herdsmen, is still a vivid recollection.

As academic children, we felt somehow unplaceable in the outside world. Besides living surrounded by university buildings, we were part of a small contingent of children who went to public school while many of our contemporaries were hustled off to the "safety" of private day or boarding schools. At the same time, a large number of Catholic children passed their whole educational lives in parochial schools, accentuating the divisions in the city. But my mother was an ardent believer in public education. According to her theory and practice, you sent your children to public schools and worked to make them better, and she gave the public school system of Cambridge a whirl that was not soon forgotten.

I remember once being sent home on a stormy winter day from the Agassiz School—our neighborhood elementary school—and crossing the path of the Shady Hill School students in Norton Woods, as they sloshed through the tempest to their open-air school rooms at the foot of Shady Hill. The Shady Hill School was one of the first progressive schools in the country, and to us public school children these denizens exuded an intolerable sense of their own purity and high mindedness, not to say, "specialness." Besides which, it apparently never occurred to them, being pious children of nature, or to those in charge, to close down classes just because a howling nor'easter was blowing. Instead, a merit was made of throwing windows open to the foulest weather. Fresh air was ALL in those days, believed to clear the brain, brighten the eye, quicken the imagination, and endow the most laggard scholar with a zest for learning. A falling mercury seemed only to increase the school's virtues. Such were the articles of faith of these "open-air kids." And how we despised them! Although in our heart of hearts we rather envied them, wondering if they perhaps had access to some essence denied us.

After grade school, we went on to the Cambridge High and Latin School, a solid, old-fashioned institution where children from all over the city gathered from their various ethnic enclaves. It was a true melting pot: Yankees, Irish, Jews, Portuguese, Italians, some blacks and other minorities, and a sprinkling of academic offspring. It was an educational experience in itself.

The question of religion was always peripherally present. When we met each morning at 8:30 and repeated the Lord's Prayer with bowed heads at our desks, you could tell the Catholics from the Protestants because the Catholics dropped the phrase, "For thine is the Kingdom, and the Power and the Glory forever and ever, Amen." The Jewish students had their holidays and seemed somehow exotic and outlandish, and no sooner had school begun in September than they had three or four days off for Yom Kippur. For Lent, girls and boys were always "swearing off" or "giving up" something toothsome for the duration, like Tootsie Rolls or Eskimo Pies, and ending up with "new outfits" for Easter. We careless little heretics never gave anything up, and I think we felt a bit left out, not partaking of this annual rite. There were no new bonnets either, as concern with clothes for Easter was considered a vestige of some idolatrous past.

After a dim week of school and homework, Saturday was the big day in our lives, and we started early in the week to brainwash our mother into allowing us to go to the movies in Boston, where we favored the Loew's State and Orpheum theaters. She would seem intractable, but by Saturday noon she would have usually capitulated, worn down by our pleading. Off we traipsed to drool over Clara Bow in *It* and weep crocodile tears over her performance in *Wings* (considered educational, therefore worthy, because it was about airplanes). I recall with some amazement what alien territory Boston seemed to us provincially raised children in the 1920s. Going into Boston was indeed an EXPERIENCE! To have known anyone who LIVED in Boston was the height of the exotic! I was much amused many years later to hear from friends raised in Boston that Cambridge was to them as remote and alien a territory, hardly ever ventured into, until some brave soul crossed the river to go to Radcliffe.

The college course at Cambridge High and Latin School was filled with bright, aspiring students determined to make their way in the world; academic child or not, one had to fight tenaciously to keep in the contest. After the demands laid on us by hard-driving teachers and schoolmates, it was a pleasure to get to college where the pace seemed relaxed. For the girls of my family, there was never any college except Radcliffe. The family could not afford any institution "away," no matter how much we may have yearned for Bryn Mawr or Vassar. But more importantly, to have deserted Radcliffe would have been a kind of rebuff to my mother.

All sorts of changes were taking place at Harvard in the late twenties and early thirties. President Lowell had inaugurated the House System, and splendid buildings were being erected along the Charles River to house the undergraduates in unparalleled comfort and luxury. In the process, there was a certain amount of cannibalization of real estate, and ladies who ran boarding houses for students were done out of their livelihood. The relationship between "town" and "gown," always edgy, took a distinct turn for the worse. Some of the awe and respect with which the university was viewed in earlier days by the rest of Cambridge had soured, and Councillor Toomey, at a meeting of the City Council, even called for a sundering of relations between the City of Cambridge and Harvard.

The student body had grown over the years and become more cosmopolitan. Professors, whose lives had seemed cloistered and parochial, were breaking out of their molds. Numerous young instructors of economics and government and some senior professors were beginning to trickle down to Washington to work in President Roosevelt's New Deal. The brightest law school grads followed, to serve as clerks to Supreme Court justices like Brandeis and Frankfurter. This trickle became a flood during the Second World War and has continued unabated ever since.

The Business School was a community unto itself, sealed away from the rest of Harvard in its neo-Georgian compound and despised by the intellectual snobs across the Charles. For them, it was a "trade school." As for the Massachusetts Institute of Technology, that was impossibly remote, a cold classical pile in the middle of a matrix of down-at-the-heels factories in the nether regions of Cambridge, where students learned to build bridges and experiment with wind tunnels, a far cry from the genteel world of the classics and the more esoteric humanistic disciplines. Academia meant Harvard, and that was that.

In my days at Radcliffe, Harvard professors still trudged across the Cambridge Common to repeat lectures delivered in the previous hour to male students in the unpolluted classrooms of Sever Hall. Many a faculty birth was financed by the extra dollars earned by his or her father in these bi-weekly treks to the hinterland. There were, to be sure, certain professors who looked with horror at the incursions of women into the sacred precincts of Harvard College, even at the safe distance of the Radcliffe Yard. For example, Roger Merriman, the first master of Eliot House and a history professor, would not have been caught dead teaching a Radcliffe class.

In the handbook of my 1934 class, we were requested to wear hats at all times when we went to Harvard Square, though gloves were no longer mandated. As for the parietal rules listed in the little red pamphlet, today they read like strictures laid upon novices in a nunnery. The rigaramole attached to going to a party in someone's room in one of the Houses was unbelievably complicated. Head tutors had to be alerted, chaperones provided, and witching hours observed. The final conclusion after all this exhausting experience on the part of the "fast" girls in my class was that a male who had escaped the Harvard houses and had an apartment of his own was no longer a student but a man, so why bother with the rest!

Radcliffe was considered something of a poor relation by the other women's colleges. The chic girls went to Vassar, the intellectuals to Bryn Mawr, and the comfortably placed bourgeois types to Wellesley and Smith. At least that is the way it seemed to us. We may have been Cinderellas, but we knew something our haughty stepsisters did not. We were getting the best education in the country and, besides, we were not banished to the sticks to rusticate. Weekends at Yale and Princeton may have been the answer to a maiden's prayer at Vassar, but we did not wait for ceremonial weekends for our entertainment. There were those among the Harvard population who recognized our merit.

This was the time of the gentleman's C at Harvard among certain prep school graduates and "clubbies," who treated the "greasy grinds" with contempt and avoided Radcliffe women at all costs. Some of us, too, were rather hierarchical and snobbish in judging our classmates. Concentrators in the sciences were thought rather "wet," and taking a laboratory course was something to be avoided for it meant long hours in the late afternoon and a freezing walk home or to one's dormitory in the winter twilight. In our carefree approach to the whole subject of education, convenience rather than intellectual stimulus seemed to have been the basis for a good many courses. Nine o'clocks were taboo, eleven o'clocks desirable.

The aesthetes frequented the Fogg Museum, and the intellectual elite concentrated in history and literature, overseen by a remarkable group of tutors, including Perry Miller, F.O. Matthiessen, and Kenneth Murdock, who created an atmosphere of excitement for generations of students. The emphasis in literature seemed to have been on English authors. If one read Evelyn Waugh's *Decline and Fall* or *Vile Bodies*, or dipped into Max Beerbohm's *Zuleika Dobson*, it was a true sign of sophistication. French literature was pretty much an uncharted terrain, and the unexplored territory of the Russian novel was as immense as the steppes themselves.

Sociology was an academic stepchild, and psychology was considered a minor pseudoscientific discipline not much discussed in those days. We who took Sidney Fay's course in modem European history emerged imbued with the idea that the Germans were not solely responsible for the First World War, a revolutionary thought we digested with a certain amount of skepticism. Our bible was the *Testament of Youth*, by Vera Brittain, which we read with an appreciation of the author's courage and valor that we longed to emulate. Its theme fitted well with our firm conviction there must never be another war and that, of course, there never would be. So deeply was this concept instilled in us that in spite of Hitler's rise in Germany, the Japanese invasion of China, the Spanish Civil War and all the other signs of international anarchy, when the Second World War finally broke out, it seemed absolutely inconceivable,

I was fortunate to travel to Europe in the summer of 1933, after my junior year, crossing like many students on the Holland

America Line. There were four classes, as I recall: third, tourist, second, and first. Third, an upgraded name for steerage, was for immigrants and impoverished students. By paying an extra $25 one could step into the exalted milieu of tourist class. I shared a tourist cabin one summer with two Vassar girls all of us en route to the École des Beaux-Arts in Fontainebleau, outside Paris. The Vassar girls at first rather intimidated me, as I had an exaggerated idea of their sophistication and worldliness. But the glamour evaporated when we found ourselves squashed into an inside cabin, sharing the joys of other people's seasickness, overflowing suitcases, and snoring. Many years later, the author Mary McCarthy informed me that my cabinmates were the inspiration for two of the characters in her 1963 novel *The Group*. Such are the bizarre items one collects along the way in a long life.

Four acolytes of Frank Lloyd Wright were aboard, simple-seeming Wisconsin farm boys fresh from the chores of Taliesin and worshippers at the shrine, something the master apparently exacted. In after years, I often reflected that these simple souls, whom I patronized so superciliously, probably went on to design some of our most distinguished skyscrapers and grandest public buildings.

There was always the chance traveling by ship in those days of meeting "one's fate," as we used to say, giving ocean voyages a particular frisson. Not that it ever happened to anyone I knew, but at least old-fashioned romance wafted through the air. If the pickings looked slim in tourist, the sport of the trip was to sneak up to first class where movie stars and millionaires disported themselves. Second class, through which we had to pass, never seemed worth our attention, amateur gold diggers that we all were! After seven or eight days of flirting, bridge, late nights around the bar, and general sleeplessness, we disembarked at Southampton, without meeting our fates, and took the boat train to London.

We spent our first night in a dreary bed-and-breakfast establishment in Bloomsbury featuring spotted white table cloths in the dining room, dried-up bacon, grilled tomatoes, slices of cold toast standing in a tarnished silver rack and strong tea for breakfast. Those were the days before Virginia Woolf put Bloomsbury on the map for visiting Americans. There were no worshipful pilgrimages to Tavistock Square, just de rigueur visits to the British Museum and the Elgin Marbles and to the National Gallery, and a ride along the Strand in a double-decker bus as far as St. Paul's Cathedral.

Then it was off to France and Art!

My two Vassar cabinmates and I shared a room high under the eaves of the wing of the Palace of Fontainebleau at the right of the courtyard as one entered the front gates. Our room was on the top floor, with an arched ceiling of gray stone and a floor of unglazed red tile. These rooms must once have been inhabited by servants or lowly courtiers, but for all that they were charming in proportions, with whitewashed walls and pale blue painted paneled doors. No obnoxious liver-colored wallpaper hung there, one's usual fate in the French pension bedrooms in which I had stayed on my first trip to France with my family. We had three dormer windows with sills so wide that we sat on them of a Sunday morning and watched French families, father, mother, two children, all dressed in black and white and starched, like figures in an Henri Rousseau painting, promenading along the gravel paths leading to the English garden.

Once a week, for a precious two francs, we commanded a hot bath in the one bathroom at the end of the corridors. As for our housekeeping, I could not say that it had improved very much since our bivouac on shipboard. We waded through heaps of discarded clothes, shoes, pajamas, newspapers, drawing paper, and letters each morning before a cheerful maid, with whom we practiced our elementary French, came and restored order.

Café-sitting in the evening was a delight. Coming from a strictly non-alcoholic family, I never learned to drink the way many students did, therefore missing out on some delicious wines and liqueurs which might have come my way. Instead, I gorged myself on French pastries and *chocolat* and by some miracle of youth did not turn into a balloon. We used to linger at the corner bar, conveniently situated across from the palace, until the witching hour of midnight when the side gate to the palace grounds clanged shut at the dot of twelve. Like a veritable phalanx of Cinderellas, we rushed to beat the deadline and then took the marble staircase two steps at a time.

On Sundays, we rode our bicycles down the country roads leading out of town, once going as far as Moret to have lunch with the proprietress of the Hôtel de l'Université in Paris, where my family and I had stayed when my father was an exchange professor at the Sorbonne. Her country house was like a miniature château painted by that ubiquitous recorder of bourgeois French life, Rousseau. It was made of sepia-colored brick and stone, with little jutting balconies and a tall slate-roofed tower topped by an iron finial. Luncheon was served under the fruit trees of the orchard beside the house. The scene was positively Renoirish, with busty ladies and overdressed gentlemen. The dappled sunlight played over the white-clothed table, replete with cold fish mousse, salad, sweet butter, peaches and plums, and chilled bottles of white wine. Even my French proved adequate, since conversation was kept at a simple-minded level in what seemed to me exquisite consideration of our stumbling incompetence in the language.

Mme. Nadia Boulanger, the renowned teacher of such American composers as Aaron Copland and Roger Sessions, was the presiding genius of the school. Her music students practiced from early morning until late at night on the first floor of the palace wing. Their pianos, violins, cellos, oboes, and French horns produced a delicious cacophony of sounds. The only other noises were the murmuring voices of French tourists and the boom of guns from a nearby school where French officers and young men did their military service. To be sure, one morning when I was walking over to the studio wing of the palace, a mustachioed Frenchman exposed himself to me under the archway. But being a "sophisticated woman of the world," I thought it was just an old French custom and went on my way. Otherwise, all was tranquil and peaceful.

Whereas the music students were an intense and dedicated group, driven by the force of Mme. Boulanger's overwhelming personality, we art and architecture students were a relaxed lot and feckless by comparison. We had our own atelier in another wing of the palace, a room almost one hundred feet long with a lofty ceiling and tall windows overlooking the Carp Pond, in which flourished enormous fish, fed by small armies of French toddlers with tidbits from the family table. Beyond lay the formal French gardens with clipped hedges and mathematically defined gravel walks. We artists took trips into the countryside to paint haystacks and village churches and sit in new-mown hayfields, in absolute quiet, except for the distant farm sounds of mooing cows and crowing cocks. And we bicycled through the Forest of Fontainebleau, identifying ourselves with the painters of the Barbizon school.

The art stores on the Left Bank, which we often visited on our expeditions into Paris, held a special fascination. Shelves reaching to the ceilings were lined with bottles of dry pigment; crocks bristled with brushes and pens. There were boxes of Conté crayons and sets of pastels, drawers of oil-paint tubes and cakes of dried watercolors, rolls of Belgian linen canvas, enormous wooden palettes of swooping design hanging from pegs in the walls, canisters of modeling tools, calipers, wooden manikins with articulated knees and elbows and feet and hands, and drawers full of handmade papers, watercolor papers, tinted charcoal papers. The voluptuous feeling that must overcome a glutton on entering a pastry shop had nothing on the sense of riches and pleasure on coming into one of those Left Bank stores. You felt part of a great tradition even though your purchase was a single sheet of paper, a bottle of sepia ink, or a steel drawing pen. But with what nicety the nib was selected, the feel of the paper assessed, and the ink held to the light to calculate the color. No French master could have used more care or scrutinized the alternatives with closer attention!

I had gone abroad in the first place to attend the Geneva School of International Studies, with only a short stopover at the École des Beaux-Arts. So in late July, after saying a sad farewell to my fellow artists and musicians, I took the train to Geneva. The proverbial saturnine Romanian shared my compartment and proceeded to advise me to fall in love while I was in Geneva, "since it heightens all the subtleties and makes one sensitive to the spirit and atmosphere of the place." Not that I disagreed with him, but I was apparently to keep my eye out for some Swiss baker's boy or the like, as he did not seem to think that the object of my affections made any difference. He then harangued me for asking such a mundane question as how high above sea level Geneva was, inveighing against my intellectual shallowness in collecting mere facts when emotion and sensation were the important things in life, rather an interesting thought for one brought up by a mother who gloried in concrete facts. At least I was learning about various facets of continental seduction.

The school was run by Professor Alfred Zimmern and his "mad" French wife, a professional pianist. Professor Zimmern lectured in the morning on international relations, and, in the afternoon, there were moribund discussion groups on sanctions, mandates, and the like, and lectures by transient scholars. According to my letters home, I found the professor's lectures "mildly interesting" and the discussions "enough to send one into a deep, deep sleep." In the evening, Mrs. Zimmern got in her licks, using music to teach her conception of international relations. She obviously disliked Americans although they were the source of much of her bread and butter. She agreed with my Romanian philosopher that all Americans were superficial and spoiled and in constant need of artificial stimulation, and that the world was going to the dogs because of these same Americans. She belonged to an ancient line of critics who believed that only art and music could save the world, and as far as I was concerned, in her quixotic way, she was right.

Art and music at that point were determining my world, and I quickly made tracks back to Fontainebleau, leaving behind a "lot of ga-ga Smith and Amherst undergraduates, who make crass generalizations about the mediocrity of America as compared to Europe and who still argued over who is better, Ruth Chatterton or Greta Garbo!" This last apparently was the ultimate put down in my lexicon. So I returned to Fontainebleau to sing twelfth-century chansons and religious music under the formidable baton of Mme. Boulanger, and, on a final outing, to travel to Chartres to paint the towers of the cathedral and delight in its magnificent stained-glass windows.

Alas, all too soon, the Second World War would break out, once again proving the Mrs. Zimmerns of this world mistaken. Mistaken she might have been, but it was at that point that I knew that I wanted above all to be an artist!

—2—

The 1930s in China and New York City

EVEN IN THOSE ANCIENT DAYS, members of the Radcliffe College class of 1934 dreamed of careers. However, only a handful went to graduate school, and most of my classmates got married on graduation, usually to worthy graduate students whom they dutifully put through medical school or law school, working for a pittance as researchers or secretaries. The height of the career aspirations of those who eschewed domesticity was perhaps to be a researcher on *Time* magazine, while a job at Macy's was thought to be rather glamorous and gave one the chance to live in New York, an experience considered de rigueur among certain of my classmates.

When I finished Radcliffe in 1934, the question immediately arose: "What shall Marian DO next?" My sister Wilma had married John King Fairbank, a budding China scholar, and they were living as students in Peking. Since I was known "to be good at drawing and painting" and had a somewhat alarming appetite for the exotic, what more logical step than to send me for a year

John and Wilma Fairbank, Shanxi Province, 1933

to the Far East and expose me to Chinese culture? I would of course have to delay my mandatory year in New York.

My brother-in-law, John Fairbank, a tall, handsome South Dakotan, had come east to Phillips Exeter, graduated in 1929 summa cum laude from Harvard, and won a Rhodes Scholarship. At Oxford, he had immersed himself in the study of Chinese history, and he was now in Peking to research his thesis on the history of the Chinese Maritime Customs Service, a peculiar institution established in 1854 after the humiliating defeat of the Chinese in the Opium War. In the peace treaty, the Western powers had forced the Emperor to allow foreign traders into China and to hire foreigners, mostly British and American, to administer duties on goods flowing in and out of Chinese ports. John had arranged to spend a few months visiting the so-called Treaty Ports of the South China coast, from Shanghai to Canton, working in the files of British and American consulates on any documents existing after decades of termites, mold, and neglect.

The plan was that I should join him and Wilma in Shanghai and that my sister and I, dutiful handmaidens, would serve him as secretaries, copying out any passages he chose to record. It gave a virtuous raison d'être (always necessary in my family!) for an extraordinary trip that began for me in the fall of 1934.

Travel to the Orient was still something of an undertaking in those days. The Dollar Line steamships took seventeen days from San Francisco to Shanghai, on top of four and a half days on the train across the continent, "changing in Chicago." These were great days for travel. "Being seen off" was a time-honored ceremony: champagne in one's stateroom in first class; for us in tourist, special delivery letters, telegrams, boxes of candy, and baskets of fruit with cellophane wrappers and gaudy ribbons. The band played on the promenade deck, the tugs tooted and the great foghorns blasted, as the huge liner pulled away, snapping the colored paper streamers we had gaily thrown to friends on the dockside. The ship headed out through the Golden Gate into the sun-kissed open sea. It was like a gigantic children's birthday party.

And so the voyage began: first the covert glances at one's cabinmate, with whom two-and-a-half weeks of intimacy were to be shared, then the agony of seasickness overwhelming all other emotions, followed by the ineffable joy of recovery. One got used to the nauseating smell of unaired saloons, the banality of shuffleboard, and the endless games of bridge. After five storm-tossed days, the wonder of beautiful, unspoiled Honolulu made it all seem worthwhile.

As I remember the ship, there were missionaries, traveling salesmen, marines returning to their China bases, stunning storms at sea with water smashing over the prow in great white bursts of spray, a casual purser who became more casual and tipsy with every passing day, and the returning Chinese, pleasant, discreet, and imperturbable among the rest of the passengers. Above all, there were the endless discussions of religion with my Southern Baptist cabinmate. She was a scrawny, wiry little evangelist, twenty years old, who had received a "call" to missionary work six years before. Her mission was at last to be fulfilled. And though she had never been outside her little Georgia town, she had set her plain but blissful face toward China, in the sure faith that she could save heathen souls for Christ. Not until many decades later did I once again see that beatific expression, this time on the face of a niece who had become a born-again, charismatic Christian.

In fact, the missionaries were the most numerous group on the boat. Being a skeptical Unitarian and a youthful cynic, I was armed and prepared not only against their fundamentalism, but, having read Somerset Maugham's short story *Rain*, I knew of the pitfalls awaiting young women and amorous clerics on slow boats to China. When a very amiable and attentive middle-aged Episcopal priest proposed that I would be a splendid bride for one of his sons, I felt sure there was more to the overture than met the eye. I began to enjoy the role in which I cast myself as the siren with whom the frustrated, impassioned man of the cloth was helplessly infatuated. It was a blow to discover that the suggestion was genuine, although the son offered up was only a junior at Yale (a further jar). Or was it genuine? The father, a humorous and perceptive man, apparently remained undisturbed by my subtle wiles. Or did he? Perhaps he was signaling in some esoteric way, too rarefied for me to comprehend. I shall never know, but I hope there was at least a flicker in his platonic heart.

The *President Hoover* finally steamed up the Whangpoo River late on the seventeenth evening of the voyage, threading its way between ghostly black junks and little sampans darting like dragon flies among the ships anchored in the blotchy waters. We lay off the Bund until morning when John and Wilma came aboard, whisked me through customs, and carried me off through the teeming streets to their "apartment." They believed in cheap living, and their rooms in a scabrous old building on the corner of Shanghai's Broadway and 42nd Street had all the appearance of an opium den.

To add to the feeling of proletarian squalor, the first guests to come for tea were the ineffable Agnes Smedley, whose Communist adherence was well known, and her friend Randall Gould, editor of the *Shanghai Evening Post and Mercury*. Since I had rather an exaggerated view of the "dedication" of Communist adherents, whose lives were supposedly devoted to "isms," it was a shock to discover that Miss Smedley's whole conversation was taken up with petty backbiting and radical gossip. In fact, it was no different from any other trivial gossip except for the damning of the Trotskyite "wreckers" and the virulence of the character assassination. The religious absolutes of my gentle, if relentless, fundamentalist missionary had nothing on the radical dogmatism of Miss Smedley. It was interesting that China should have been the country in which these two exemplars of fanaticism found such rich soil to till.

It was a memorable introduction to the "exotic East," but only one facet of a great and turbulent city. The riotous streets swarmed with rickshaws, carrying whole families, the fleet-footed drivers moving deftly amongst streetcars, buses, and the sleek limousines of wealthy Chinese and foreigners. Exquisite society women and cocottes, ablaze with their jade and diamond jewelry, thronged the lobby of the fashionable Cathay Hotel. The grandest building on the Bund, the British Consulate, shone with polished brass railings and doorknobs and gleaming mahogany furniture, although the building was pervaded with the faint odor of mold, the proverbial smell of the Treaty Ports. Here John worked within the sober halls and offices, unraveling mysteries in the consular documents.

We had Thanksgiving in an elegant house in the French Concession, our host, a "simple" academic, obviously living "the good life," waited on by a retinue of amahs, bearers, and servants.

His Downstate U. was never like this! And one Sunday we were taken by a friend to the house of an ancient scholar whose Sunday morning relaxation was the painting of bamboo scrolls, an art of which he was the most famous practitioner in China.

Most poignant and horrifying was a visit to a silk filature factory in the poorest section of the Chinese city: two hundred women and children working in one room, sorting silk cocoons and removing their outer skins with only a dim light trickling through a doorway and a row of filthy windows. The enormous room looked like an obscene rat's nest, writhing with humanity and smelling like a thousand unwashed feet. Children as young as five and six years and women with nursing babies worked away, as overseers patrolled with switches in their hands, striking recalcitrants. The hours were four in the morning until six at night, the children earning about two cents a day.

Upstairs, little girls were standing in billowing steam, stirring cocoons in boiling water, while other girls led off silk thread onto drying racks. Expressions of dumb resignation blighted the girls' faces. The skin on their hands was white and macerated and eaten away. The wretchedness of the scene was unimaginable. Such dreadful and heart-rending examples of industrial serfdom and exploitation were no doubt repeated over and over again behind the glittering facade of the metropolis. From the abject misery of such enslaved men, women, and children, the forces of Communism and Maoism gained strength and flourished.

Our travels took us by boat from Shanghai to the remoter ports of the South Coast: Foochow, Amoy, Swatow, and on down

The Chip Sing *to Foochow, c. 1934*

to Hong Kong and Canton. Sailing the coast had its hazards in those days, as pirates infested the waters between Shanghai and Foochow, our first port of call. Before our departure aboard a raffish, rusting vessel named the *Chip Sing*, officials discovered a stack of smuggled rifles in steerage. Some men claiming to be bodyguards to a Foochow general had allegedly carried the weapons on board under their clothes. I remember the screaming of the men and the violence of the Shanghai police as the offending passengers were removed, protesting all the while that their general "needed an arsenal."

It was somewhat reassuring that heavy steel plates with peep-holes to shoot through separated the bridge and the cabin passengers from steerage. In addition, our fortress was patrolled by a fierce-looking Sikh with a huge mustache, a turban, side-arms, a scimitar, and a heavy rifle, though his musical comedy appearance was perhaps not entirely convincing. The steerage deck overflowed with passengers: women with nursing babies and bound feet (always a shocking sight), toddlers, and groups of men gambling, spitting, and fighting. Adding to the confusion were the quacking and honking of ducks and geese, bursting out of their raffia-and-reed baskets, and the squealing of shackled pigs. It was a wonder that small children did not slip under the railings into the heaving, yellowish sea.

There were five cabin passengers: John, Wilma, myself, a missionary school teacher, and a young German Jewish art historian. We sat cozily in a tiny cabin, drinking the particularly strong Indian tea served wherever England held dominion. I have always wondered what happened to the art historian who chose to wander through the remoter parts of China discreetly picking up old paintings and scrolls. He had the eye of a connoisseur and may today be the owner of a great collection. Or he may have returned to Hitler's Germany and been liquidated, though even in such a brief encounter, one sensed in him the qualities of a survivor.

On the afternoon of the second day, we entered the mouth of the Min River, surely one of the most beautiful rivers in the world, snaking between misty, craggy mountains; and after sailing past this awesome scenery for two or three hours we finally dropped anchor in Foochow. So many scenes come to mind from that far-distant time, memories of people and of a kind of life that even then was becoming archaic. This once thriving port of call for British and American clipper ships of the China tea trade in the nineteenth century was now a deserted backwater. Lofty colonial mansions, with deep verandas and poinsettia hedges, were clustered together on the hills, recalling the port's opulent past. From sandy paths meandering past the high-walled gardens of these mansions, one could see far in the distance the Chinese city and the river. A charming, neo-Gothic Church of England chapel—built of the local stone and musty with disuse—stood under an enormous camphor tree, and in the graveyard stood the pathetic headstones of sailing captains, missionaries, women and babies, dead of cholera or the plague or of hearts broken by loneliness, poignant reminders of death in an alien land.

The oldest inhabitant was Mr. Brand, the teataster, who ran the seedy boarding house in which we stayed. Like a grand seigneur, he presided over a crumbling, gray brick mansion, pointing out with pride every tortured knickknack, fat black Buddha, or carved Chinese pagoda choking his salon and describing their provenances in excruciating detail. Immortalized by Somerset Maugham as a rumpled colonial in one of his short stories, Mr. Brand had come out as a clerk from the Midlands some forty years previously to work for the trading firm of Jardine Matheson. In those forty years, he had never returned to England, and he had never learned to speak a word of Chinese, communicating with his middle-men and servants in ugly pidgin English.

At the end of the day, Mr. Brand regaled us, his captive

audience, with a variety of hour-long recitations. With his long, greasy, gray hair hanging to his shoulders and one hand laid on his expansive stomach, while gesturing with the other like a revivalist preacher, he intoned "The Fireman's Marriage" or "The Death Scene from Henry VIII," by W. Shakespeare. Both works seemed to carry the same weight in his repertoire. In another age, he might have been a mediocre actor doing a turn in a provincial music hall.

Besides histrionics, Mr. Brand's great pleasure in life was his aging English wife, a cheerful, buxom woman of strong personality, who faithfully played the role, assigned by him long ago, of a simpering female. He once led me by the hand into their bedroom so that I could admire her as she sat in a tatty dressing gown on the edge of their colossal bed and brushed her waist-long hair. Gray and faded though it was, Mr. Brand exclaimed, "Look at her hair, how long it is. How thick. Isn't it beautiful, beautiful!" and fondly spread out the hoary locks for me to see them better.

Husband and wife went together each morning to the office in the huge *godown*, or warehouse, littered with bills and papers and with brass spittoons placed in strategic spots. A pallid young clerk, lately arrived from England, wearing an eyeshade, black paper cuffs, and elastics hiking up his shirtsleeves, scratched in a bulky account book with a steel pen. Shadowy figures of Chinese servants moved about in the background as Mrs. Brand, her large bosom encased in a black office apron, sat at a desk performing on an ancient clackety typewriter.

One morning, Mr. Brand introduced me to the mysteries of

Temples in Foochow *by MCS, 1934*

teatasting, which took place in a high-ceilinged room next to his office where some two thousand canisters, containing samples from hundreds of tea gardens "up-country," lined the walls. A Chinese aide poured out six cups of boiling hot tea, which were allowed to stand for a few minutes in delicate porcelain cups. In his role as expert teataster and irrepressible ham, Mr. Brand, with flourishes and pirouettes, raised each cup to his lips, sloshed the tea around in his capacious mouth, and then spit the mouthful out into a battered tin basin. The clatter and rattle of his false teeth struck a singular note to the process. The aide placed the tea leaves on individual plates, and Mr. Brand examined the leaves for texture and color, identified their source, categorized their quality, and, with a ceremonial wave of his hand, dismissed the business of the day.

From the tea tasting room, he took me into the enormous *go-down* where hundreds of gaily painted tea boxes were piled up, waiting for shipment. The smell of this room was a pungent mix of the smoky scent of tea, the faintly acrid exhalations from the dry bamboo slats and reeds of which the tea boxes were woven, and an underlying odor of mold, dust, and decay. Outside the great doors, the river ran swiftly. Gorgeously painted sampans and hulking junks floated by, and the bustle and cries of river people, who lived and died on boats in the murky water, made a perpetual babble.

I remember the beauty of the river women, with their steel-black hair worn in elaborate coiffures, secured by highly decorated silver barrettes and barbaric hairpins, and with their feet unbound. They were still to be seen dressed in loose black pajamas and jerkins, swinging along the Foochow Bund under the ancient camphor trees, babies slung on their backs or flat baskets balanced on their heads, with all the grace and pride of a race of Amazons.

The foreign community in Foochow was a paradigm of all the tiny, inbred groups huddling together in the largely bypassed ports of South China. Social demarcations were rigid. Mr. Brand and his wife were strictly of a lower order when it came to the consuls, the bank manager, and the customs commissioner. As for the missionaries, they lived a life apart, like oil and water, hardly ever mixing with the official community. In all, there were fewer than one hundred foreigners living in the city.

As I wrote in a letter home:

> We dined with the American Consul. We dined with the
> British Consul, and enjoyed the mutual backbiting. We
> dined with the Customs Commissioner, and the head of the
> Hong Kong Shanghai Bank, etc. All these are English and
> I was surprised to find them so friendly and outgoing. I
> guess their reputation for snobbishness has been exagger-
> ated or maybe they are hard up for new faces. Wilma's and
> my reference to an interest in art and Chinese antiquities
> cast an aura about us. John's esoteric thesis subject and
> Oxford connections are absolutely devastating! And so we
> float happily along, passed from hand to hand. And then,
> yesterday, we went across the river in a sampan to have
> lunch with Mr.---, a missionary who teaches at Fukien
> Christian University, and got the other view. He is a great
> connoisseur of Chinese pottery, and the house was so full
> of shards there was hardly room to sit down. He is a manic
> collector and one feels that his poor beaten-down wife and
> children have been denied new shoes and clothes so that he
> can feed his passion. And the Niagara of his talk gave me a
> whiff of how Sinologues react. At least the missionaries are
> in touch with the Chinese, which is more than can be said
> about most of the foreigners living in Foochow.

Almost every afternoon, my sister and I set out with our paints
and watercolor blocks to sketch. One quickly learns that sketching in "underdeveloped" countries has its perils, not because
people are hostile, but because they are so friendly and curious.
The Chinese were no exception. They apparently found us irresistible, for not only were we "foreign devils" but women besides!
It was hazardous to try to paint from the quays, as the crowds
were so dense that we were in danger of being flung bodily into
the water by the sheer pressure of five hundred kibitzers. The

Buddhist temples were safer, somewhat removed from the crush of humanity, though the white robed monks with their shaven heads proved to be unabashed, giggling onlookers.

The temples themselves were gorgeous, with sweeping, exaggeratedly curved roofs, paved with brilliant yellow tiles, and with blood-red plaster walls, characteristic of architecture in South China. From time to time, the ringing of the deep-throated temple bells would break the stillness of the courtyard where we sat painting under some enormous ginkgo tree. After the clang and clamor of daily life, the quiet in these beautiful old temples was almost deafening. I often wondered why a seemingly unmystical people like the Chinese should produce so many monks and came to the perhaps frivolous conclusion that retiring to a remote monastery was the one way to escape that country's perpetual noise and overwhelming mass of humanity.

Many of these monasteries clung spectacularly to the sides of sacred mountains and were the objects of pilgrimages, where the sick, the blind, the sterile, and the mad ascended the winding trails in search of salvation. My sister and I climbed Mount Kushan, towering over the valley of the Min River. Stone steps, worn by the feet of thousands upon thousands of pilgrims, twisted and turned for miles through sparse pinewoods. We passed the derelicts of humanity along the way. No painting by Hieronymus Bosch could have prepared me for the pitiful cripples, the horribly disfigured, and the pathetic old people, dragging themselves like mindless ants to some dreamed-of deliverance. It was like Lourdes magnified a thousand times, a memory of China I have never forgotten.

After Christmas and New Year's in Amoy, a sleepy port on a small island off the mainland where we made our usual progress from Chinese fleabag to consular mansion, we arrived in Hong Kong.

Hong Kong was still very much the outpost of Empire. Gentlemen in white flannels played cricket on perfectly manicured lawns; ladies dressed for tea in wide brimmed hats and gloves, and the "inscrutable Chinese" were no more than eerie shadows moving in the background. The capacity of the British to carry their culture with them wherever they went was never more evident. We ran up against it in the form of British colonial officiousness a day or two after our arrival. We were summoned before a pompous British police sergeant for having failed to register within eight hours of our arrival, confronted with our crime, and treated like case-hardened delinquents, until wily John produced his impressive collection of letters of recommendation. Like so many colonial types, the police sergeant, so firm, so immovable, so legalistic, was enough of a snob to let us off, though not without an insufferable lecture on "ignorance of the law" being "no excuse," as though we were a trio of reprobate schoolboys. Our address was probably a source of some suspicion in the eyes of the Hong Kong police, for in our quest for cheap lodgings we had ended up in a Chinese hotel that turned out to be a brothel.

One afternoon the bellboy knocked on the door of our room. "Velly much like the young leddy," said the bellboy, obviously the house pimp, who was representing his client, an eager counterpart of an American traveling salesman, standing on tiptoes behind him. My sister and I had been swishing through the corridors in our bathrobes to the only bathroom, which in those surroundings had obviously been considered a come-on. We were both duly affronted, though I somewhat complacently felt that the young lady spoken for must be me. My brother-in-law rose to the occasion and with a remarkable display of trumped-up outrage and self-righteousness dispersed the pair, thereby causing them humiliating loss of face. The desk clerk must have thought we were pretty peculiar customers when John called up the management to complain in "horror." After all, why the fuss? Wasn't the gentleman traveling with his two concubines?

No sooner had we hit bottom in the back alleys of the city then, like waifs transported by some fairy godmother with a magic wand, we were whisked up the funicular to the Peak. The usual process of being passed from hand to hand that operated in those days throughout the Far East was functioning again, and this time we attained a state of grandeur well beyond our normal desserts, in the mansion of William Johnstone "Tony" Keswick, head of Jardine Matheson, Ltd., the oldest and largest British trading firm in China. John wanted to examine the firm's old documents, and Mr. Keswick generously invited us to stay in his huge house on one of the highest points of the island.

In the afternoons, after a stint among the dusty archives, we sat and had tea in the salon beside a coal fire, while Mr. Keswick did needlepoint and gossiped with his friend Gerald York. York, a quasi-journalist, was a lanky "long drink of water," as the phrase used to be, a typical Oxonian of the thirties, with long greasy hair falling across his eyes and clothed in floppy gray flannels well spotted with samples of last week's menu. He was the master of one-upmanship and was forever at the scene of the latest event in China "when it happened," before "anyone else"! He had just appeared in "dear Peter's" (Fleming's) travel book, *One's Company*, and there was much malicious gossip about Ian and Harold and Peter, to everyone's mutual satisfaction.

At other times, we watched the sunset from the veranda, with its entrancing view of the harbor alive with junks, ferry boats crossing to Kowloon, sleek gray British gunboats, and British merchantmen with LONDON lettered on their stems, standing at anchor or taking on cargo from lighters. My memory went back to the signs on the warehouses along the Thames's docks and the shiny brass plates on the grimy office buildings in the City announcing the names of trading companies and limited partnerships dealing in hemp from Calcutta, coconut oil from the South Seas, and tea from China. I was reminded of English novels in which younger sons were forever going "out East" to seek their fortunes in Hong Kong or Singapore. Here was the reality, for it was from trade carried on in these distant outposts that so many fortunes were made which were the foundations of Victorian prosperity and British self-satisfaction.

But the deterioration of British mercantalism was already far advanced, as we had seen with Mr. Brand, and we had caught glimpses in Amoy and Swatow of the privileged life of the British colonial, soon to be in precipitate decline. In less than five years, the Second World War would begin, administering the coup de grace to an outmoded, anachronistic way of life. Looking back, it seems that we viewed it all like amateur anthropologists coming upon an exotic tribe that we had read about and felt lucky to see before its final extinction.

———

It was at the start of the Chinese New Year when we took the train north from Shanghai, leaving behind the lush rice fields, elaborate temples, and fantastic mountains of the south, and crossing the sere north plains to Peking. All along the way, blue-clad families stood outside their adobe-walled houses and waved as we passed. The children made spots of color in their holiday best, brightly flowered jackets and trousers, the girls' hair braided with magenta ribbons, the baby boys wearing embroidered shoes and tiger caps which warded off the evil spirits. Pasted on the doors were red paper cutouts of gods, and an occasional multicolored kite streaked the brilliant blue sky. Otherwise, all was dun brown: houses, rutted roads, frozen fields, leafless trees.

The year 1935 probably marked the beginning of the end of the old way of life in Peking. The Japanese, occupying large territories in Manchuria, were preparing further incursions into China proper. That spring, skirmishes took place only a few miles from the city. Within two years, the Sino-Japanese War would break out in earnest, with all its ramifications and portents for the future of China. So we were fortunate to see the old city in its tattered medieval splendor, with its people still living much as they had for hundreds of years. What luck to have glimpsed the ancient past before the onslaught of twentieth-century know-how, politics, economics, and wars obliterated it forever.

The fascination that houses have held for me all my life was richly rewarded on my Chinese travels. In addition to the

stunning mansion on the Peak in Hong Kong with its marvelous harbor view or the raffish boarding house of the teataster
in Foochow, there was above all the charming house in which
the Fairbanks lived in the East City in Peking. It was a typical
Chinese house, built around two courtyards, with the entrance
way opening onto a dusty lane or *hutung*. In spring a canopy of
wisteria festooned a part of the main courtyard, and a whole
garden of narcissus, brought in shallow baskets on the shoulders
of a passing street vendor, was planted in narrow beds lining the
pavement of the court. The air rang with the sounds of bicycle
bells and the calls of street hawkers, water bearers, coal sellers,
and sweetmeats men, signaling their presence to householders
sequestered behind high walls. The creak of heavy two-wheeled
wagons piled with bags of millet or rice and drawn by scrawny
horses echoed in the narrow lanes. One morning, I stepped out
the front door and ran headlong into a large Siberian camel from
the Western Hills, laden with baskets of coal for the Fairbanks'
stoves.

Although my sister and brother-in-law were allegedly pover-
ty-stricken students, their full complement of servants consisted
of Li, the head boy, a cook, an amah, and a small boy, a relative
from an outlying village, who had somehow been inserted into
the household. The cook was a troublemaker and a petty tyrant,
taking more than the usual increment of squeeze from every financial transaction, so that there was a good deal of wrangling
from the kitchen area where these four resided with a virtual
army of family hangers-on.

But in our courtyard all was peace and serenity. Each morning,

John, a tall blond figure sensibly garbed against the winter chill in a heavy, padded, blue gown, retired to his study on one side of the courtyard. There, surrounded by Chinese texts and character cards and attended by his Chinese teacher, he attacked this impossible language. My sister, an art historian, worked on her restoration of rubbings in another cubbyhole. And I, in the dining room, facing on the courtyard, took my morning painting lesson with the elegant Mr. Teng.

My vocabulary of a few well chosen "haggling" words was all right for bargaining. Bargaining was the breath of life to all Chinese merchants no matter how small the transaction, and I would have lost disastrous face if I had ever bought anything at the asking price. But it was not the idiom of art. I soon discovered that the idiom of art required no words. Mr. Teng's gracious bowings and smiles were enough, and we were soon on the best of terms. He carried his art materials carefully wrapped in a blue-gray cloth. Each day he laid them out on the dining room table as though setting up for an elaborate banquet. He lined up six or seven brushes of different sizes in perfect order on one side and arranged the ink stone and ink block on the other. The rice paper was in the middle, precisely squared with the brushes, and central to the geometric design, a copy of *The Mustard Seed Garden*, an ancient manual containing the entire vocabulary of strokes from which Chinese paintings are created.

With many smiles and many encouraging "hao's" (good), a few "boo hao's" (not good), and a lot of "hao boo hao's" (is that good?), we plunged along. He taught me how to hold the brush (always perpendicular to the paper), grind the ink (always clockwise), dip

Sword Dancer *by MCS, 1935*

the brush, place it on the paper, and maintain the rigid order of strokes ordained since time immemorial. No classical ballet was more stringently or precisely ordered, or seemed more effortless in its final effect, than the great Chinese landscape paintings. Mr. Teng sought to teach me the basic rudiments of philosophy and technique behind them. I was running fast to keep up, as he took me over the threshold of this ancient art, taught me to draw plum blossoms, tree peonies in spring, mountains in a winter rain, gnarled pine trees, ginkgo trees, water running over rocks, bamboo stalks in the wind. Each had its ordained vocabulary of strokes. It was like studying harmony and discovering the underlying elements on which concerti and symphonies are built. Forever after, I looked at Chinese paintings with a new eye.

Street Toy Seller, *illustration from San Bao and His Adventures in Peking, by MCS, published 1939*

Every stroke was meaningful. The almost architectural planning and building of the great Sung scrolls and paintings were a source of wonder.

The huge walls surrounding Peking still stood as they had for hundreds of years, crenellated and pierced at intervals by enormous gates through which flowed the clamorous traffic of the metropolis. I walked along the footpath atop the walls and looked down into hidden courtyards and temples. At certain points, I could see an overview of the gridlike plan on which the city was built. At the center stood the Forbidden City, with its fortress-like red walls and gold tiled roofs. The Communists tore down these great walls some years ago, thereby destroying one of the most awesome architectural relics of China's past.

While the cold weather lasted, Wilma and I rode our little Mongolian ponies across the frozen fields that began beyond the sluggish moat that surrounded the city walls. We stopped and exchanged greetings with the villagers in their tiny hamlets, my sister in her fluent Mandarin, I in the always reliable language of smiles. We admired their babies, their pigs, and their geese, and wondered silently at the grotesque maiming of the women with their bound feet. Though the barbaric practice was against the law, the custom still prevailed among the peasants in their remote villages where age-old traditions determined the destiny and fate of women, not government dictum.

Some years later, inspired by the memory of these glimpses of village life, I wrote and illustrated a children's book, *San Bao and His Adventures in Peking*, about a small boy from the countryside who goes to the city. It was a vehicle for recording the sights that I remember so vividly: street fairs with jugglers and acrobats, old gentlemen airing their caged song birds, wrestlers performing in temple courtyards at New Year's time, noodle sellers and sword dancers and so much more.

Of an evening my beau, John Davies, a Foreign Service language officer connected with the American Embassy, and I used to go to performances of Chinese Opera. I would take along my drawing block and pencil in the hope of doing sketches of some of the performers. It turned out to be a hopeless task in the face of the riotous earsplitting noise of the music and the actors

Actor from the Chinese Opera in Peking *by MCS, 1935*

Party at the Great Wall, 1935

storming around the stage while attendants flung hot towels to the patrons sitting enthralled, noisily cracking sunflower seeds and spitting shells on the floor. In later life John Davies, along with other able China Foreign Service officers, was denounced, harassed and persecuted by the McCarran Committee during the McCarthy period, blamed for "having lost China," a ridiculous concept typical of the hysteria of the times but lethal in its effects, bringing many innocent people's lives and careers to ruin.

With our friends we often packed our bedrolls, wrapped up a few cans of food, beer and evaporated milk, and set forth on expeditions. It was a great land for exploring with lovely Buddhist temples in the Western Hills, the Ming Tombs, and the Great Wall. A rattletrap car might take us part of the way. Then we would proceed on foot, hiring a donkey or two to carry our baggage. There was always a little teahouse along the way for refreshment, for no matter how far afield we wandered there were always people.

One weekend, a party of us danced Scottish reels on the Great Wall—perhaps on the very site of Nixon's sanctified stroll almost 40 years later—and laid out our camp rolls in a tower or under the stars, forewarned to douse our campfire before going to sleep lest it attract the attention of bandits. But inevitably, out of nowhere, a couple of Chinese soldiers appeared and took up guard duty on our behalf. The next morning they cheerfully accepted a tip and built us a fire for our morning tea. One thing was certain—in China, you were never alone!

After my Chinese adventure, having experienced the wider world and finding it to my taste, I set forth to make the obligatory assault on New York City. Despite the glories of Macy's and *Time* magazine, I looked in other directions for a job with some connection to the Far East. I was lucky to find a position as a research assistant at the Institute of Pacific Relations in its rabbit-warren-like headquarters on East Fifty-Second Street. Three weeks after my arrival, when I was consulted as an "expert on China" by one of those "exotic" girl researchers from *Time*, any thought of joining the publication as a female slavey evaporated.

The atmosphere at the IPR was strictly egalitarian. There were perpetual staff meetings at which all employees, from lowliest secretary to executives, visiting Oriental scholars, wandering students, and fresh faced researchers, were soberly consulted on every policy decision, no matter how trivial or how weighty. Everyone was on a first-name basis, and the position of women was equal, if not superior, to that of the male. In a peculiar way, many of the characteristics of the 1960s were manifest. The big-happy-family, all-proletarians-together approach was emphasized to a self-conscious degree. In fact, the IPR was populated by powerful women, and the patrician figure of Frederick Vanderbilt Field, executive director of the American Council, was like that of some classical youth surrounded by a troupe of Amazons.

We wrote articles, helped edit *The Far Eastern Survey,* read the *New York Times* and the *New York Herald Tribune* at our desks, held earnest talks on the telephone in answer to earnest queries, worked up statistics from the *Japan Year Book* (apparently our sole source book), and yawned a good deal at the fecklessness of our labor. Considering that the IPR was accused during the McCarthy era of being a devious institution that corrupted a whole generation of China experts and was instrumental in "losing China," I often reflect that our chief emotion at the time was one of futility. Some of us loudly complained that no one paid any attention to the blameless articles we wrote or helped to edit for *The Far Eastern Survey* and *Pacific Affairs.*

It was the depth of the Depression and the height of the Popular Front, and there was a political fever in the air that was a new experience for me. It was palpable as one walked the streets, went to the movies, ate in restaurants, a kind of desperation, which one felt in the hard-pressed counter boys, harried waitresses, street beggars, and men and women shivering in the frigid streets of mid-winter Manhattan. Many of the IPR staff were political activists; some, I realize now, were members of the Communist Party or devoted fellow travelers. Hardly an evening passed without someone rushing off to a conference or meeting devoted to left-wing causes. I often tagged along, attending dinners for Earl Browder, head of the Communist Party USA, and fund-raisers for the United Mine Workers and the Congress of Industrial Organizations. One was always finding oneself at a party or gathering where furious political debate was taking place between Stalinists and Trotskyites.

I remember attending a rehearsal of the left-wing revue *Pins and Needles*, presented by members of the International Ladies' Garment Workers' Union in a loft in the garment district. I felt enlivened by the energy, brashness, and spirit of the performance and delighted by the music of Harold Rome, though doubtful about the simplistic political message. I recall sitting in the balcony of the Fourteenth Street Playhouse, listening to the hortatory words of Clifford Odets' *Waiting for Lefty* and *Awake and Sing!* and not quite being able to share the emotional fervor and identification embraced by the rest of the audience. It was exhilarating but at the same time faintly ludicrous. The skepticism of my upbringing would not be downed. The isms and absolutes, as well as the sentimentality of the fellow travelers and party-liners, seemed unrealistic, dehumanized, and phony. I could never get used to the way "the people" so often came out as abstractions or statistics to be manipulated for political purposes. In fact, the whole experience was a basic introduction to the crudeness of "politics."

On the other hand, I remember seeing Clare Boothe Luce's *The Women*, which seemed extremely daring and sophisticated, and Lillian Hellman's *The Children's Hour*, which I thought the most brilliant play. It was supposed to be about lesbianism, I was told. I was pretty vague about what lesbianism meant, but there were certainly tensions and overtones in the play that even I could not miss. It was the days when Radclyffe Hall's *The Well of Loneliness* was one of the great underground books, and after seeing the play we sought it out for further illumination.

In the meantime, my roommate and I lived a kind of subterranean life in a cockroach-ridden, one-room apartment a block off Washington Square. It seemed to consist of one long hall with two grubby windows giving out on an airshaft, a sordid kitchenette in a closet, and a daybed that opened up into two hard pallets. The first one of us to bed got the one with the springs. It was a typical disastrous choice of two neophytes, but it was cheap and we did not know any better. We were fair game for all our visiting friends, who strung along the hallway, head to foot, when they spent the night. An especially tall Australian, six feet six, once monopolized the total space from front door to the so-called living area, and for a week I stumbled over him to go to work, as Australians appeared to be nerveless, heavy sleepers.

I was forever rescuing my roommate from the clutches of un- wanted boy friends whom she seemed to attract in her forays uptown on the subway to the Juilliard School where she was studying voice. They would come to the door or call on the phone, and I would deny any knowledge of anyone by that name, an exercise in white-lying that I never mastered. Once when she unguardedly agreed to go to dinner with one pathetic specimen, I rushed to the restaurant by prearrangement and announced in hushed, tense tones that a long distance telephone call had come through. "Your father is deathly ill, and you are called home immediately," I whispered loudly in a transparent performance. It was a sad little subterfuge all around. But we thought ourselves very clever.

My roommate did not last long, but I seemed made of sterner stuff, for I stayed on to live in various exotic haunts, including a small room at the back of a children's theatre in the East Thirties, where I stumbled through the spooky drops and scenery for *Hansel and Gretel* to reach my tiny bedroom. It was not a setting to inspire confidence, but I took it as a challenge, feeling that if I could beat down my fears of papier-mâché hobgoblins, I would be armed against the world.

In the summer of 1936, I attended the International Conference of the Institute of Pacific Relations at Yosemite. Delegations from the United States, Japan, China, the Netherlands, the USSR, England, and France gathered under the great spruces of the valley floor for roundtable discussions, while low-level functionaries like myself acted as recorders, secretaries, and errand-runners. Our bird's-eye view was informative. The British were always earnestly caucusing "in committee," while the French seemed to take their duties rather lightheartedly, spending a good deal of time playing bridge in their elegant suite in the Ahwahnee Hotel. There was a good deal of drama in the course of the conference. Not only did the Spanish Civil War break out, but also the Moscow trials began. There was the moment when Vladimir Romm, U.S. correspondent for *Izvestia* and a member of the Soviet delegation, was called back to Moscow, to what he must have known would be his fate, for he stood trial and was later liquidated. The Japanese were represented by the military and by officials (read "military") of the South Manchurian Railway, as well as by members of the government that in a few months would launch an all-out war against China.

I wrote to my mother: "It is curious how electric the air gets when the Japanese are even indirectly concerned in the discussion. They are in a terrifically touchy state of mind, and apparently incapable of approaching the problem of their place in the affairs of the Pacific in an objective light. There are four or five unidentified Japanese thugs who hang around who I am sure are spies."

I remember a scrub baseball game between the Japanese and American delegates, a typically informal contest in which the contrast between the Japanese and American players was remarkable. The Japanese were intensely serious and determined to win, while the Americans fooled around, perfectly willing to give the Japanese a break when they lagged behind, lest a loss precipitate an international incident. In a way, it was the beginning of the end, for in a very few years the roles played by most of the participants suffered cataclysmic changes, and the issues and questions that we so earnestly discussed had long since become academic.

3

Guatemalan Odyssey

ANOTHER HOUSE QUICKENS my memories. This is a long, low, whitewashed ranch house, draped in fuchsia bougainvillea, its red-tiled roofs glinting in the tropical sun, on a huge coffee plantation in Guatemala. Nestled on the slopes of the live volcano El Fuego, the *casa* sat in a lovely garden shaded by a towering *matapalo* tree and overrun by a flock of screeching guinea hens and a pair of proud, puffed-up peacocks. And the *corredors* were alive with the chirping of caged birds and grumbling saucy parrots. But to go back ...

It was the fall of 1938. Hitler and Chamberlain were about to sign the Munich Pact, establishing "peace in our time" and the Spanish Civil War was drawing to its bloody, tragic close. I remember listening to one of Hitler's violent harangues on the radio in Cambridge during that hectic September and, without understanding German, feeling the fanaticism and hatred in his voice. I remember scanning the peaceful skies of a perfect New England autumn with nothing but slow-moving biplanes idling from time to time across the empty blueness. The people of my generation, though curious and horrified onlookers at Hitler's brutality, generally adhered to the fundamental belief that there would never be another war, at least one in which we would be involved.

It was by the merest chance that I went to Guatemala that fall. While traveling by boat from Los Angeles to New York through the Panama Canal, my parents had met the Pettersens, who owned a coffee plantation in Guatemala. It became an immediate and enduring friendship, especially between Carmen and my mother, inevitable that they should like and appreciate each other for they were both free spirits of great independence and energy. Carmen was a painter, a watercolorist of distinction, who over the years had recorded the brilliant costumes of most of the Indian tribes in the country. When she suggested to my mother that I come and stay at the Finca El Zapote for a few months and paint, the decision was quickly made. It was characteristic of my mother that she would ship me off to stay with people I had never met, in a country I had never heard of. And I guess it was characteristic of me that I fell in with her plans without a murmur.

Travel to Guatemala was made on the sleek boats of the United Fruit Company as they made the round trip from New York to pick up cargoes of bananas in Guatemala, stopping along the way for a day in Jamaica. From raffish Porto Barrios, reminiscent of all the backwater ports ever described by Joseph Conrad or Somerset Maugham, one took the narrow-gauge railway that meandered through the banana plantations on the sultry, steaming coast up into the highlands where Guatemala City is situated.

Guatemala City was a small dusty place in those days, not yet a tourist mecca, with most of its side streets unpaved and one less-than-Grand Hotel, where the *finqueros* from the outlying coffee and cattle *fincas* gathered to gossip, drink, and do their business when they came to town. It was like an unfinished, frontier metropolis in the early days of our Far West, with the Indians in glorious costumes down from their remote highland villages for the weekly market and, dominating everything, the brilliant sunlight of the tropics and the magnificent purple volcanoes of the near horizon.

My host and hostess had boarded the train at one of the stops a few miles outside the city, and any apprehension I might have had disappeared in the warmth and enthusiasm of their greeting. Pete, a sandy haired, energetic Norwegian, had come out to Guatemala as a young man, leaving behind his beloved fjords to seek his fortune in this exotic land. Here he had met and married Carmen, whose vitality and pioneer spirit matched his own, and they had put down roots, establishing one of the most beautiful and prosperous coffee plantations in the country.

For two days, we stayed in the city in the house of Carmen's parents, themselves early "pioneers" and rich characters. Like so many men at the end of the nineteenth century, Carmen's father had left England to seek his fortune, first in Mexico and then as a coffee broker in Guatemala. Now retired and stone deaf, he was a good-looking man with a flat-top brush of white hair and a square, craggy face, who sat most of the day on the sunny patio, reading and growling to himself, sometimes smacking his jaws together like a snapping turtle.

Carmen's mother, a pretty, round figure with dyed black hair done up in tight ringlets, a coquettish pink or magenta ribbon planted in their midst, and plump fingers with rings, seemed not to have gotten it through her head that her husband was stone deaf. Though she shouted at him in a perfectly natural way, he never heard a word, which did not stop him from shouting back in a loud voice. Frustration would finally impel her to write out her questions on any convenient scrap of paper, which she handed to him, prompting an even more violent outburst in ever richer and more stentorian tones.

Her absent-minded cheerfulness expressed itself in other bizarre ways. She had a habit of tucking her false teeth down her bosom and, when reminded by her chauffeur where to retrieve them, broke into floods of lighthearted giggles at her stupidity. She was said to prefer hanging her pearls around the neck of her little dog rather than giving them to her daughters. She always described her aches and pains, of which she seemed to have a goodly number, in terms of the shapes of geometric figures, especially triangles and diamonds. She had never learned to speak English fluently, and she often told funny stories on herself in her atrocious English, a literal translation from the Spanish, ending in deep-throated laughter at her barbarous linguistic distortions. Her childlike qualities expressed themselves in a passion for sweets and bonbons, which no doubt contributed to her ample contours, and in a love of building, for she was the architect of her eccentric house, which resembled an edifice erected out of children's blocks. In fact, the house was only partially finished, awaiting the inspiration of the mistress as to how a half-built and largely irrelevant staircase was to connect to the second floor.

On the third day, we set off on the long drive to the *finca*. The plantation lay half-way up the flank of the volcano El Fuego, which had in the past erupted violently from time to time, sending rivers of hot sand and ashes down its slopes, gouging deep valleys and sharp clefts, destroying roads, and obliterating buildings. The tortuous road we drove upon dipped down into these chasms, ran across streambeds of black volcanic sand, and skirted gigantic boulders thrown up by the eruptions, the landscape resembling my idea of the surface of the moon. Having climbed out of the last of these *barrancas*, the road emerged into a more beneficent landscape with lush fields of sugar cane stretching toward distant hills and the Pacific Ocean and pastures where Brahman bulls and cows grazed. Rising in the north was El Fuego, brilliant and sharply defined in the clear air, with a wisp of whitish steam lazily drifting from the cone. At last, we entered an avenue of royal palms, and under an enormous ceiba tree a gate opened onto a cluster of whitewashed *finca* buildings with red-tiled roofs arranged around a huge open floor on which pearly gray coffee beans lay out to dry.

I slept in the annex to the big house and woke up to the murmur of running water in the brook that meandered beside the open porch off my sparsely furnished room. In the main house, they awoke to the squawking of peacocks in the garden behind the house and the screeching of guinea hens in the leaves under the *matapalo* tree. In the early morning, too, the *peóns* began their daily tasks, raking coffee beans back and forth over the cement drying floor, rolling them over and over to better expose them to the sun. Adding to the general chorus, the blue and orange parrot screamed in the *corredor*. And so the day began. We ate breakfast in the *corredor*, shaded from the brilliant sun by a screen of potted hibiscus, which also separated the drying floor from the *casa*, though the sound of scraping rakes was a reminder that this idyllic spot was the center of large-scale agriculture.

By breakfast time, Pete, my amiable Norwegian host, had long since disappeared into the *beneficio*, the large whitewashed building on the other side of the drying floor, next to the entrance gate. Here was the office where the records were kept and telegrams sent and received, and where, if you were lucky, you could have a scratchy telephone conversation with someone in the outside world using an almost prehistoric instrument. And here Pete conferred with his German manager, a scrawny young man, who, with the rise of the Third Reich, had become a devoted Nazi. His pale blue eyes had a fanatical gleam, and such was the rigidity of his stance that you could imagine his giving the Nazi salute with the same ardor as a devout Catholic might cross himself in church. Having been told by the German minister in Guatemala City that the Führer had pronounced it the patriotic duty of all good Germans to buy a Volkswagen, he had obediently purchased a VW bug, the first I had ever seen. The presence of this young zealot was a thorn in the side of my hosts, since both Carmen and Pete were staunch anti-Nazis. But they were for the moment stuck with this rather pathetic man and his equally pathetic wife, about to bear her first child for the Führer.

I remember sipping our coffee at the table in the *corredor* and listening to the latest horrors over the radio, broadcast by the BBC Overseas, as well as to the closing prices on the coffee exchanges in New York and New Orleans. There was something unreal about our after-dinner ritual around the shortwave radio with its static sometimes deafening and the high-pitched, cultivated voices of the BBC announcers fading in and out, as the high winds swirled around the towering volcano interfering with reception. In the silences, you heard the distant jangle of the *marimba* from the *ranchos* of the *finca* workers at the end of the dusty road beyond the avenue of royal palms.

I had arrived at the end of the harvest season, when the last of the crop was being gathered. Ox-drawn carts overflowing with cargoes of red coffee berries lumbered past the *casa* to the huge coffee barns. The sound of the great machines processing the berries, separating the red outside flesh from the gray beans, rumbled from morning to night, as an army of men, women and children, some native to the *finca*, others contracted to come down from their highland villages, spread out through the *cafetale*, trudging along the grassy paths between the coffee bushes, filling their baskets with the glossy fruit. One heard the murmur of their voices and their soft footfalls late in the afternoon as they passed down the lane to their *ranchos* and their evening meals of tortillas and black beans. On Saturdays, they gathered at the loading platform of the *beneficio* to collect their wages, which consisted primarily of rations, corn and beans. Very little cash was handed out.

Guatemalan Indian *by MCS, 1938*

Often in the evening, at sunset, we would sally forth from the coolness of the *casa* and sit on the wall surrounding the drying floor, to see the glorious pink clouds surging up around the cone of El Fuego and watch the chimney swallows sailing on the wind above the *finca*. It was splendid to observe the perfect rhythm of the swallows' flights as they caught the wind, dancing and playing with it, until at last their leader plummeted straight down into a deserted chimney of the coffee barn with not one of the following birds missing the mark.

One settled soon enough into the tempo and routine of the *finca*. Carmen and I often drew from models: small girls dressed in their best brilliantly colored *huipiles*, their glossy black hair braided with orange or purple ribbons; sober men, in dark brown serapes and white trousers, somehow extracted from their usual labors by the irrepressible Carmen. Or I set off on a sketching expedition to draw the leaves of the breadfruit trees or scenes from the weekly market under the branches of the ceiba tree by the front gate. My sketch book was full of drawings of the pet *pizote*, the red and blue parrots swinging on their perches, the men raking the coffee beans, the cone of El Fuego, oxen dragging heavy carts, women balancing baskets of fruit on their heads, little naked children playing in the dust, and the two Great Danes snoozing on the cool tile floors of the *corredor*. It was grist to my mill, for I would use many of my drawings as illustrations for a children's book, *Children of the Fiery Mountain*, which I wrote after my return from Guatemala.

When there is a flowering in the *cafetal*, the spicy scent of the little white flowers of the coffee bushes is perhaps the most intoxicating perfume in the world. We often rode horses through the *cafetal*, through this heavenly scent, to the upper annex of the *finca*, high on the flank of El Fuego, where Pete was experimenting with growing cinchona, the plant that produces quinine. We made the expedition to Monte Rey, as the place was called, as often as twice a week, since many plant experts and curious, unidentified persons with letters of introduction dropped in to see how the plants were growing and whether it was feasible to raise cinchona in the American tropics. We suspected that some of our visitors were agricultural spies sent by Dutch companies, which had the world monopoly in the Dutch East Indies. There were

Finca El Zapote *by MCS, 1938*

rumors that an enterprising Englishman had smuggled seeds out of the Dutch East Indies, which found their way by devious routes to this lovely Central American plantation. Whether our suspicions of spies were justified or not, Monte Rey was off limits to all but a few.

We used to sit around after these treks and talk about the day the Japanese might take over the Dutch East Indies. Then people would discover that under their noses, in the American tropics, quinine of excellent quality was being produced. But in our discussions that time was always in the remote future, far enough away so that it could be contemplated with equanimity. We thought that there was all the time in the world to watch the

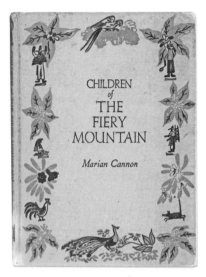

Children of the Fiery Mountain *by Marian Cannon (Schlesinger),*
published 1940

trees grow to maturity and yield their health-giving bark. Yet Pearl Harbor was just about three years away.

It was not just good business that had prompted my up-and-coming host to launch his experiment with cinchona. Pete had accepted the proposal of the directors of the pharmaceutical firm, Merck and Co., to grow cinchona because he was both a forward-looking agriculturalist and a passionate patriot. Although he had lived much of his adult life in Guatemala, he remained devoted to his native Norway.

Sometimes when we got up early in the morning to ride to Monte Rey, we passed on the trail the wraith-like figure of a man running down the path as if his life depended on it. He never acknowledged our presence and went by in utter silence. His was a pathetic story. He had been sent out from Switzerland, where he had studied as an architect, persuaded by an uncle to replace a cousin who had died of snakebite while administering a small *finca* in the remotest part of the country. There he was forced to stay for three years without ever coming out. And there he apparently went to pieces, losing all connection with his former life and any hope of returning to Switzerland, having been abandoned by his callous uncle and virtually penniless. He became involved with an Indian woman and had two children by the time Pete took pity on him and hired him to manage the upper *finca*. All he could do in fulfillment of his desolate life was to run down the long trail from Monte Rey to the lower *finca* and back, and this he did every morning. To run up and down the side of the volcano must have given him some touch with the mountains of his native Switzerland. Such mournful stories abounded of broken lives and suicides of European "pioneers" living on isolated plantations in the backcountry.

Christmas came and went with all its pageantry and religious ceremonies. Rockets went off and bells rang at midnight when the Virgin was said to give birth in the little whitewashed village church set under the pine trees across the drying floor. There was dancing and merry-making in the square in front of the church. It was a joyous occasion and the noise was frightful. Almost everyone got drunk. Tiny boys took their turn at the marimba, in wide black brimmed hats like their elders, and children lay asleep all over the place. In the morning, as all the servants had long since collapsed of drink, the son of Geronimo, the majordomo, reported that "my father is decomposed and can't work today."

People dropped in at all hours to partake of the hospitality and open-handedness of the Pettersens. Some arrived on business, like the representatives from Merck and Co., sophisticated-looking men in well tailored suits, checking out the cinchona plantings. The Norwegian minister put in an appearance from time to time, a crafty old soul given to pinching the Ladino girls and deceiving his wife, who stayed in the city. A stunning woman named Nora Planck, married to a ne'er-do-well husband, would arrive from the city with her small blonde daughter to stay a few days. She invariably brought along a minute Indian child, the daughter of her cook, a dark and silent little creature who was treated rather like a puppy, to be played with and then dismissed when not wanted.

Nora's history was a twisted and tragic one. She had been adopted from a Chicago orphanage by the president of a small Central American republic and his wife and brought up in so-called luxury in the presidential palace. Then her father had either been overthrown or died, and she had had to make her way in the world alone. She was a handsome, passionate young woman, blonde, with vivid blue eyes, but with a vile temper and a venomous tongue. I think she despised her husband as a weakling, much less intelligent than she, but attractive. They were rather an F. Scott Fitzgerald pair. She drank heavily and, I was told later, died of alcoholism. When I knew her, we would sit with Carmen on the *corredor*, gossiping about the latest scandals in the city, about people I did not know but whose lives and peccadilloes as described by these two past masters of reportage were fascinating. Nora had style and brains and felt keenly the deprivation in living in what she considered a dusty, hopeless backwater. I think she found comfort in Carmen, who for her part embraced her *finca* life with enthusiasm and involvement.

Like so many people who live on plantations, Carmen was an ardent collector of plants and trees, exchanging seeds and cuttings with like-minded neighbors or friends as far away as Jamaica and Costa Rica. The *finca* was renowned for the opulence of its flora and its bird sanctuary. In the evenings hundreds of white herons and green parrots flew in from the coast and roosted in the trees surrounding the four or five man-made lakes.

Carmen was always busy. She was the local doctor to whom the women of the *rancho* brought their babies for medicine or advice, almost a daily task. She taught her daughter at home before she went off to boarding school. She painted the native costumes of the Guatemalan Indians, wrote letters to her many friends, and oversaw the running of the household and the training of the simple Indian girls who served as maids in the *casa*. She saw that the *pisotes*, the dogs, the peacocks and the guinea hens were fed. She rode her horse through the *cafetal* with the rest of us and arranged that I should set off to see the great ruined city of Antigua and the Indian villages of the highlands before I returned to the United States.

And so, one day, I set forth, my paints and watercolor blocks stored in a brightly colored saddlebag, my wardrobe consisting of a shirt, a sweater, a pair of jodhpurs, and a pair of riding boots.

I took a ramshackle bus, which stopped outside the *finca* gate, with the usual accompaniment of squawking chickens in wicker baskets, trussed ducks, and black-eyed children with silent mothers and fathers squashed into every inch of space en route to the weekly market in some miserable local hamlet. After a bone-splitting ride over appalling roads, we reached Antigua, where I gratefully got down and made my way to my hotel, an enchanting inn created out of an old colonial mansion. Carved wooden shutters still adorned the windows, wide teak floorboards were buffed to an elegant sheen, ancient fruitwood chairs were arranged stiffly around the second-floor *sala*, and the only other guests were Osbert Sitwell, the English aesthete and poet, and his boyfriend.

I was interested in the ponderous wooden "gout box" which Sitwell's companion carried around by its heavy handle and into which he helped his portly charge thrust his gouty foot. It seemed a wonderfully Victorian contraption, an example of medical practice appropriate to the likes of Osbert Sitwell. I suppose it served some soothing function of which I was unaware. I always regretted that shyness kept me from opening a conversation with the pair, but I enjoyed the minor dramas that took place as they sat in the *sala* of an evening or in the patio of an afternoon, the irascible Sitwell nattering peevishly at his mincing caretaker.

Antigua, which in the seventeenth and eighteenth centuries had been the capital of the Spanish Empire in Central America and rivaled Lima and Mexico City in wealth and population, was virtually destroyed by a series of devastating earthquakes in

1773. The city that I saw, a beautiful little sleepy relic with many of its streets grassy paths, was an undiscovered treasure, a gem. Its lovely, white gleaming churches, those that still stood after so many disasters and some in ruins, were embellished with amazing garnishes of baroque angels, rococo scrollery, classical pediments, winged putti, madonnas and saints in ornate niches, all of unbelievable detail and elaboration. There were said to have been more than one hundred churches in Antigua at the height of its wealth and power, each enriched with these fantastic sculptural facades. One had a sense that the Spanish Catholic padres and their superiors in the New World, freed from any inhibitions of their native land and having at hand inexhaustible supplies of virtual slave labor in their Indian captives, had gone mad in an architectural frenzy and built, built, built!

In the late afternoon, I strolled through the *paseo* in the middle of town where the courting went on, the men walking in one direction and the girls in the other, giving each other a thorough looking-over. And at noon, the prostitutes repaired to a room across the hall from the post office in one of the arcaded buildings lining the plaza. They received their customers during the lunch hour, a dirty old bedspread serving as an inadequate door, rather a public performance that nobody seemed to notice. Quite an education for me when I happened in to mail a postcard to the family!

Carmen was a planner who believed that I should see and have every experience of the country. She arranged that I meet a young man, Jack Harman, in the plaza of Chichicastenango, in the highlands, and go on a pack trip with him into the back

Guatemalan Woman at the Marketplace *by MCS, 1939*

country, a trip he made annually to contract for the labor of Indians living in villages over the mountains toward Petén. It was the usual thing for *finca* owners to hire seasonal laborers to make the long trek from the highlands to help pick the coffee crop for the two or three months of the harvest. I had never met the young man and had only the vaguest idea of what I was getting into, but Carmen, always the optimist, assured me of his character. So heigh-ho, you only live once, on with the romp!

Early one chilly morning in the pitch black, I set forth on

another laden bus, trundling over narrow dirt roads, swooping down steep *barrancas* and up over steep hills, stopping at every little Indian village along the way. In each, the men and women wore their distinctive costumes, some ravishing magentas or deep reds, others purples, pinks and oranges. By the time I reached Chichicastenango, the sun was already high, and I sat luxuriating in its warmth on the steps of a small church, sketching the great cathedral across the square. I was the only foreigner in the vast plaza and certainly the only lady sketcher for miles around, so there was no question as to my identity, or his, when Jack drew up in his car. Needless to say, I had never seen my assigned companion before, and after a good look I decided that everything would be all right.

He was rather a dashing figure in shiny riding boots, a bush jacket, and a rakish sombrero, which he doffed in a playful gesture, revealing a humorous face. With a puckish grin, he introduced himself. He had been forewarned, for Carmen told me he had caught a glimpse of me at her parents' house in the city the day we arrived and had apparently liked the cut of my tweed skirt and the color of my Jermyn Street shetland sweater. He was obviously a clothes snob!

Without further ado, we drove until dark across the rolling countryside on narrow, twisting roads, stopping every once in a while to explore some remote church or drop by some miserable shop in a tiny hamlet, where a few cans of sardines and some bottles of orange soda, grimy with age, were the only goods on the shelves. The road was a well-worn one for Jack. After going to prep school in America, he had left the giddy life of a playboy in

New York to take charge of the family coffee *finca*. His Spanish was fluent and his relationship with the Ladinos and Indians with whom he chatted along the way was easy and friendly, full of jokes and banter.

When we reached Sacapulas, by the Rio Negro, long after nightfall, the only illumination came from dim oil lamps giving out a wavering light through the open doors of a bar and a fly-specked inn. A few donkeys and bony, undersized horses with tattered bridles were tied to a railing on a plaza with a ceiba tree spreading its huge branches over hard-packed dirt ground. The murmur of men's voices and an occasional bray from one of the burros were the only sounds. But the sparse meal of evil-looking scrambled eggs and black beans tasted good, and the stark beds, boards with crib-like shallow sides, did not keep us from sleep in our dusty clothes.

At midnight, we set forth, ensconced in wooden saddles on two scrawny horses, in order to travel before the heat of the day. The full moon sailing high in the west was our only light as we crossed the Rio Negro and began the long climb to the Santa Abelena *finca*. As we went over the pass commanding a sweeping view of the lush jungles stretching towards the Petén peninsula, we witnessed a remarkable and, according to Jack, a most secret rite. Two Indians were kneeling before a sort of shrine on a knoll overlooking the spectacular sea of green. Four or five crosses made of branches tied together with grass and adorned with dried flowers stuck out of the ground. Burning resin sticks perfumed the air. We stood a little below the shrine, hardly daring to move, feeling like interlopers at some hallowed sacrament. The sun was filtering through the branches of the lofty pine trees overhanging the site, and the scuffling of a large bird through the underbrush was the only noise to break the deep silence.

Watching this ceremony of returning home, I thought of the men's back-breaking labor on the *fincas* and the miles and miles they had walked or trotted with heavy packs, carrying blankets, food, cooking utensils and machetes up from the coast and over the mountain, and I sensed their heart-felt thanks for a safe return to their Eden-like homeland. The Indians prayed but no sounds came from their lips. I felt their intense identification with the land, which had been theirs long before exploitation had reached into these remote highlands.

We arrived at Abelena in the late afternoon. The ranch house consisted of two large rooms on either side of a large hall, with thick whitewashed adobe walls and a minimum of furniture—a chair or two, a crude trestle table, and two shallow box-like beds, all cobbled together by the local carpenter. While Jack conferred with the overseer, contracting for a certain number of Indians to come to El Quetzal to pick the coffee crop, I stretched my legs which were stiff and sore from the lamentable wooden saddle and bony-backed nag I had ridden all day. There was something deeply pastoral about the setting. The paths were green and lined with banana plants, giving one the feeling of being in a well-tended park. Thatched Indian huts clustered around the little ranch house. A spooky silence reigned. No one spoke, and even the small children seemed subdued and unusually quiet. Not so much as a nod acknowledged my presence when I attempted a

Guatemalan Woman Going to the Pila, Chajul
by MCS, 1939

friendly gesture. The Indians seemed to live in an impenetrable world of their own.

Next morning we set forth on our miserable horses under a lowering sky. Toward noon we came to the village of Chajul, where one of the most ghastly slaughters in the Guatemalan civil war would take place in 1982. I remember reading of that carnage with horror and recalling the day Jack and I rode our scrawny mounts down the grassy main street of that ill-fated hamlet. It was a strange experience, dreamlike and ethereal. I felt in a miraculous way that I had been transported to some ancient Greek agora for the women wore costumes that can only be described as Grecian: a halo of pink cloth around their heads, a fling of cloth dropping shoulder to ground, intricately patterned in muted lavenders and mauves, incorporating a motif similar to the Greek key, and long white cotton skirts. On their heads or under their arms the women carried clay water jars resembling amphoras, filled at the village *pila*. The men wore clothing of the same soft and subtle shades. It was market day, and the central plaza was crowded with men, women, and children. As the day was overcast with low-lying clouds, I had the eerie sense that the whole village might be enveloped in mists and disappear as in some fairy tale told from a mythic past. Perhaps its doom was thus foretold.

It was some weeks later that I went to stay at El Quetzal with its hundreds of coffee-producing acres and views of distant volcanoes. Jack's father was now a feeble old man who sat all day wrapped in shawls in the elegant drawing room of the *casa*. An engineer, he had come out from a small town in New Hampshire at the turn of the century to help build the railway from Porto Barrios to Guatemala City. He had been a friend of the dictator Jorge Ubico, a friendship which no doubt was instrumental in his becoming a large landholder. He seemed to have retained some of his Yankee shrewdness that had made his fortune for I think he looked on me with suspicion, as a possible seducer or fortune hunter. After all, I had gone off on a rather unconventional toot with his son, and who knew who I was?

At a rather advanced age, he had married a little seamstress from San Salvador, part Indian, part Spanish, of extremely simple background but smart and ambitious. When I met her, she was a worldly, neurotic, handsome woman with dyed jet-black hair, much corseted, much bejeweled, much perfumed, and meticulously dressed, in the fashionable black of Spanish ladies, no matter what the season or the temperature. She had a kind of domineering arrogance when it came to dealing with her servants, harshly bossing them around, and yet at the same time treating them like children, confiding in them, chiding them, taking care of them. Indeed, one sensed that her relationship with her servants was the closest one she had.

Like her husband she was suspicious of me, seeing me as some kind of adventuress in pursuit of her mainstay, Jack, who watched over everything, the *finca*, the old father, the money, the Indian workers, the marketing of the coffee, the wrangling and negotiating, the overseeing of the overseers. Later she decided that I was no threat and proceeded to confide in me. Out poured a stream of bitter complaints about her unhappy life and her useless husband. I had the feeling that she could never have enough of the world's goods, not enough jewelry or money, not enough sex, attention or love. Hers was an insatiable personality, jealous, thriving on feuds, full of a kind of primordial malevolence. There seemed to be a dark, vengeful streak running through her and poisoning her every relationship. People were afraid of her malicious tongue. And she certainly twisted the life of her son Jack. Yet I could not help liking her. She was not to be put down by life. Many years later, when I read Gabriel Marcía Márquez's novel *One Hundred Years of Solitude*, I felt I had lived for a brief moment in a milieu similar to what he described in that strangely dark and brooding volume. She had great taste. Her collection of Spanish Colonial antiques, *santos*, and paintings in their elaborate rococo frames was spectacular. Her table was laid with rich, heavy Georgian silver. Her china was Spode, and her food, beautifully served by soft-footed Indian maids, was perfection. Some time later, a friend of mine, who knew the family when they lived at one point in Connecticut, told me a charming story. The mother and daughter bought inexpensive silk dresses at Macy's, tore out the seams, and sewed them back by hand. Thus was French couture created with the minimum of cost and the maximum of effect by the clever hands of the seamstress from San Salvador.

One evening, with two or three paying guests staying at the *finca*, we were having drinks before dinner in the living room when it was suggested that we visit the *beneficio* where the coffee beans were processed. We trekked through the garden and down the path to the great coffee barn where, in the midst of inspecting the machinery, Jack's mother suddenly screamed that she had lost a diamond from her bar pin. She looked on us malignantly, as though we were in some way responsible, and excoriated the workers in the tones of a crazed fishwife, insisting that the factory be turned upside down in order to find the diamond. One would have thought she had lost the Kohinoor diamond the way she screeched. It was an embarrassing scene, as if one were present at some episode of family madness.

In the midst of the outcry, which continued with increasing violence as we wended our way back to the house to the living room, her husband slunk away and Jack took her gently by the shoulder and led her away. In a few minutes we went into dinner. There was Jack's mother at the head of the table, the perfect hostess, only once snarling at the pretty barefoot maid for her sloppiness in passing the paella. To be sure, there was a slight earthquake as we sat at table, with the chandelier waving over our heads and the wine sloshing in our glasses, and one of the guests became hysterical and had to be soothed with cold compresses. But all of this was mild compared with the eruption in the *beneficio.*

This was my weird remembrance of my first visit to El Quetzal. With it remain the memory of the flights of hundreds of green parrots streaming across the evening sky from their feeding grounds on the coast, returning to perch in the colossal trees of the rain forest, and the memory of the pungent, spicy perfume of a coffee plantation in full flower suffusing all.

Many years later, I flew with Jack over the site in Guatemala where the CIA trained anti-Castro Cubans for the Bay of Pigs invasion. All that was left to be seen in the deep jungles of the coastal plain below Quetzaltenango was a cracked cement airstrip and some collapsing tin-roofed huts, mute testimony to a reckless adventure. We made two passes but saw no signs of life. Then Jack wheeled his small Cessna to the south and set us down within an hour on the landing strip at El Quetzal. Since I had last been there, he had had a landing strip bulldozed out of the jungle. It must have been an engineering feat to build it, for the land was rugged, cut by deep *barrancas,* and huge ceiba trees and acres of coffee bushes had to be sacrificed. But with the plane Jack could go to the city in thirty minutes, a trip that had taken most of the day when I came to the plantation in a springless jeep over dusty, bumpy roads.

Even in 1967, Jack was afraid. Guatemala, ruled by dictators who violently suppressed the Indian majority, was riven by civil war. In spite of the fact that as an overseer he was a compassionate master, he knew that his life was in danger and kept a small pistol tucked in his belt. An armed guard lounged at the entrance gate some miles down the road which led to the main building. Lounged was the right word, for the stance was purely symbolic. Jack survived until the 1990s when guerrillas, wielding machetes, hacked him to death on his *finca.* But he was a fatalist and no doubt knew that one day all his good fortune would exact its toll. His life story seems a paradigm of Guatemala: compassion, exploitation, blood, cruelty, Swiss bank accounts, incredible riches, incredible poverty, unearthly beauty, awakening aspirations, the perfume of the flowering coffee bushes, the putrid odors of rotting vegetation and rotting corpses, the ancient story of the land reaching back to the days of the Conquistadors.

Church in El Quiché *by MCS, 1939*

The old ranch house that had so charmed me when I visited
more than thirty years previously now looked down-at-the-heels
and crumbling. The hanging baskets lining the *corredor,* once
containing profusions of orchids, were untended and weedy. A
slatternly Indian girl brushed the dead leaves from the tiled patio
with a twig broom. Another equally untidy girl, who in the days
when Jack's mother presided would have had her hair dressed
with magenta and orange ribbons and her *huipil* freshly laun-
dered and ironed, languidly dusted the furniture and straightened the pillows on the couch in the living room.

The painting of the church in Quiché that I did on that first
trek still hangs in my living room. I had promised it to Jack as a

wedding present, but he never married. I hope that he was buried on the high plateau where El Quetzal spreads over hundreds of acres, in the heart of the *finca* he so loved, with its marvelous views of the volcanoes and rain forests and with the green parrots flying in from the coast at evening.

4

The War Years

I REMEMBER SO WELL the first time I met my future husband, Arthur Schlesinger Jr. It was a beautiful, sunny spring morning in 1936, and I had returned to Cambridge for the weekend from New York City, where I was working as a researcher for the Institute of Pacific Relations. I was sitting in the living room when this lively, spirited, opinionated young man entered, come to take my cousin, who was living on the third floor, out on a date. I thought he was the brightest male I had ever come across and, in my so-called New York sophisticated way, thought, "Now, that is the sort of man I would like to marry, but I suppose it will never come to pass." I doubt if he in turn even knew who I was or even noticed me. But fate intervened. We met again that fall at the Tercentenary Concert in Symphony Hall, celebrating Harvard's three hundredth anniversary, and I even remember that I wore a jade-green chiffon dress for the occasion.

Arthur was the son of Arthur Schlesinger Sr., the distinguished professor of American history at Harvard. Like me,

Marian and Arthur Schlesinger, 1941

Arthur was an academic child. After graduating from Harvard summa cum laude in history and literature, he had spent a year at Cambridge, England, and on his return became a member of Harvard's Society of Fellows. In the meantime, I had written and illustrated my children's book on Guatemala, *Children of the Fiery Mountain*, which was published in time for me to present to him at our wedding in August 1940.

We started our married life in another house, this time a pretty Federal-style house with a wrought-iron balcony on Harvard

Street. On the first floor, where we had our apartment, the windows reached from floor to ceiling. As a member of the Society of Fellows, Arthur was free to do research on his book on President Andrew Jackson. I continued to work as an illustrator of children's books. Our rent was $80 a month, which seemed like a colossal sum, though helpfully augmented by a kindly aunt. But such an expenditure did not keep us from having parties from time to time, serving what we thought were sophisticated drinks of canned grapefruit juice and gin and inviting such grand figures as Samuel Eliot Morison, who arrived resplendent in his riding clothes, crop in hand, for cocktails.

The neighborhood was full of characters, dusty old landladies in their echoing mansard-roofed houses, painted a sooty gray and falling down in disrepair over the heads of equally dusty roomers. An ancient lady wearing an improbable boa winter and summer used to take her cat for an outing on a leash studded with rhinestones. Old Mrs. Gilbert, the widow of a professor of music, lived in a particularly decrepit house stuffed to the ceiling with old newspapers and magazines. With her paisley shawl over her shoulders and her layers of gypsy-like skirts dragging behind her, she freely mumbled disagreeable comments about anything or anybody that displeased her, as she hobbled along the uneven brick sidewalk. She would sally forth to attend any talk listed in the *Harvard Gazette* which might interest her, to do battle, for she seemed to look upon such public lectures as a call to arms. She would sit squarely in the front row, where she was the terror of the New Lecture Hall (today's Lowell Lecture Hall), and harangue the lecturer with sharp questions or wave her cane, demanding that he "speak up," as she could not "hear." It was her daughter Tessa, then an aspiring teenager, who made a classic Cambridge remark, anxiously asking R.P. Blackmur, the poet and critic, "Do you think I will EVER grow up to be an intellectual?"

Beautiful copper beech trees, so typical of the landscaping of the Victorian period, were often planted in the front yards of the looming Victorian houses nearby, the shade from their luxuriant leaves making the interiors even more mournful in summer. One often saw a long funeral procession of some Italian worthy, with lines of black cars and black-garbed passengers and two or three open sedans banked with floral offerings, streaming for seeming miles down Massachusetts Avenue. Nuns, walking in pairs in their habits, like black and white birds, dotted the landscape. Butter was 28 cents a pound at the local A&P. When I asked the clerk why unsalted butter cost 29 cents, he thought for a moment and said, "Probably because they have to take the salt out."

The war in Europe had begun, and across the United States a fierce debate was taking place between isolationists and interventionists, nowhere more passionately than among the young instructors and graduate students at Harvard. We despised the America Firsters, who were stupidly and dangerously ignorant of the perils of Hitlerism, and we noted that many of them were what we thought simple-minded Yale men. Closer to home, we fought the good fight with the fellow travelers among our acquaintances. One came to discriminate among one's friends by whether they were interventionists or isolationists, and the tip-off was the rapid change-over by the fellow travelers when Hitler invaded the Soviet Union in June 1941, breaking his pact with Stalin. Such impassioned interventionists they suddenly became!

I wondered then at the enslavement of people to an ideology, but after years of observing the power of cults to seduce and distort the lives of people I knew well, I realize that I was naive in my understanding. Ideological enslavement seems to be part of the fabric of the human condition, no matter what era or what circumstance.

Then came the Japanese attack on Pearl Harbor in December 1941, a stunning blow. I remember so well when the news broke. We had just turned on the radio to listen to the New York Philharmonic Concert, a fixture of Sunday afternoons, when the program was interrupted and the attack announced. It seemed absolutely unreal. How utterly unprepared we were, having been raised with the fixed idea that there would never be another war, at least one in which we would be involved. Having spent a year in China and Japan after my graduation from Radcliffe in 1934, I knew where Japan was, but there were thousands of Americans who had only a vague idea where our newest enemy came from. However, be that as it may, with the declaration of war by Germany on December 11, we were suddenly in a two-front war. A new life began for all of us.

Mrs. Botsford, our good-natured landlady, descended from her second-floor aerie, trailed by her three scruffy children, to share her excitement with us. She was in a state of exaltation as her wimpy husband seemed to have been galvanized into action by Pearl Harbor. He had taken a stand, his manhood at last on the line, and had determined to send his wife and children "inland" to Ohio or somewhere safe, to escape the Nazi bombs, while he mounted the barricades. Somehow, the thought of Nazi bombs falling on the corner of Harvard and Dana streets in Cambridge, Massachusetts, seemed remote to me, but Mrs. Botsford only simpered with delight at this manifestation of her husband's masterfulness. Cosseted at last! Of course, the Nazi threat to the corner of Dana and Harvard streets never materialized. Instead of mounting the barricades, gun in hand, Mr. Botsford went back to scrounging for a living, sent on his way by his large and commanding, not to say, disappointed wife.

That spring the street lights were dimmed, without any absolute blackout being observed. It was hard to realize that we were in a war, though friends and acquaintances began to disappear, either drafted, enlisting, or applying for commissions in the army and the navy. We went to Washington in the fall of 1942, part of a large contingent of young people taking jobs in the capital. Arthur worked in the Office of War Information. My assignment was to look after twins, Katharine and Stephen, born in August 1942. My chief memory of our arrival in the city was of a cheerful black porter wheeling the two bassinets containing the babies through Union Station, calling out, "Right this way! Two of a kind coming up! Two of a kind coming up." (Not quite accurate as they were brother and sister.)

If women think they are "stuck" with little children today, they have nothing on women in the same boat during the war. In my case, I had no diaper service for the twins for four months, no matter how desperate my pleas. Such institutions as laundromats did not exist, and I had only a sort of children's washing machine

Stephen and Kathy, 1948

that looked as if it had been invented to wash dolls' clothes. To be sure, an amiable black cleaning lady arrived twice a week to "clean," but mostly to sit with the children while she slipped me her pass on the District bus line for an outing at Woodward & Lothrop in downtown Washington or a foray to the hairdresser or the grocery store. I shudder at the memory of other "baby-sitters" we resorted to in our desperation, teenagers and even ten-year-olds, hardly out of babyhood themselves. One small delinquent, in a distorted idea of fun, scattered little tacks all over the living room floor to greet our return after an evening out.

Ration books were issued to all citizens, no matter how young, and the extra ones acquired with the twins' citizenship were a godsend, as we hoarded gasoline ration stamps for expeditions into the countryside or saved precious food stamps for certain staples often in short supply. Such a one was coffee. It was through coffee that I made my mark on the community. My friends in Guatemala had sent me a fifty-pound bag of green coffee beans as a wedding present, somewhat delayed as it arrived after the birth of the twins. I soon became the most popular woman on the block, doling out rations of beans to neighbors and friends, teaching them how to roast and grind the beans to make the most delicious coffee they had ever tasted.

It was in Washington that I began to paint portraits, especially of children. Someone gave me a small Victorian walnut frame, and I felt called upon to paint a portrait to fit it. Not only did the frame stimulate me, but I had the inspiration of a great-grandfather who had been an itinerant portrait painter in Maine. My little blonde niece sat for me. I proceeded to develop a style of my own, based in part on early American primitive portraiture with its flat, simple, straightforward delineation and, in turn, also on ancient Chinese ancestor portraiture. I had been intrigued by the many examples of these portraits I had seen when I studied Chinese painting in Peking. Again, the figures were painted in very flat colors, their magnificent robes represented in minute detail. Yet the faces, almost completely lacking in modeling, are always markedly individual. One sensed that they were very good likenesses. I have worked out a technique or style that combines the two influences: the flat, almost abstract, painting of the body, clothing, and setting, but the face carefully delineated and individualized.

In June 1944, Arthur went abroad for the Office of Strategic Services as a civilian, having applied to the Department of the

First formal portrait by MCS, 1945

Navy for a commission and been turned down as the result of the bureaucratic hysteria of the time. The powers that be had apparently confused him with his father, who had been branded a flaming "red" by the FBI for having contributed to a fund for medical relief for the Loyalists in the Spanish Civil War. The organization was listed in the FBI files as "subversive." Since Arthur Sr. was a devoted Democrat and civil libertarian, it was a characteristic smear of the period.

Having parted from Arthur in New York after a memorable evening listening to Billie Holiday sing in a smoky dive in the West Forties, I went back to Washington to collect the children and, like so many others, retire to the boondocks to wait out the war. The boondocks in Franklin, New Hampshire, were lovely in the spring. The brooks were gushing with water with skunk cabbage awash on the banks. Pushing up through fallen leaves and ground pine were yellow lady slippers seeking the sun. It was as idyllic a spot to wait out the war as one could have asked, though through the long summer and autumn the news from England of V-2 bombs dropping on London was not very reassuring.

But no disaster befell, and, as winter wore on and France's liberation became assured, the OSS office was transferred to Paris and with it, Arthur, who no sooner arrived than he was drafted into the army as a buck private. Though he was later advanced to corporal, his most exalted rank, penury still persisted, and in an effort to augment the family exchequer, I sat down and wrote a book, entitled *Twins at our House*, which I illustrated with drawings of the two children, caught on the wing, so to speak, as the twins were at that dread age of two-and-a-half when action and mobility are paramount. The book went on to a certain fame. Many years later, when Arthur's father and mother spent a sabbatical year in Holland, having been asked to tea by Queen Juliana, they presented her with a copy. Perhaps her grandchildren read it.

In the late fall of 1944, having picked all the wild grapes and gathered the wormy apples from the ancient Baldwin apple tree, the children and I moved back to Cambridge to spend the winter and spring in a borrowed apartment. On a balmy April day in 1945, I took the twins for a walk to the comer drugstore for popsicles. As we wandered home, I noticed a subdued hum of

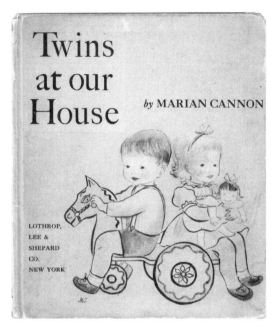

Twins at our House *by Marian Cannon (Schlesinger), published 1945*

voices, as we passed groups of people standing in their doorways and on the street corners. The news of Roosevelt's death had just been announced, and the world seemed stricken with grief and foreboding. Or so it seemed. But as I took my trash out to the back hall of the apartment, I was met by a neighbor, a seemingly blameless, mild-mannered woman, who proceeded to gloat over Roosevelt's death in the ugliest, most vicious terms. I always regret that I did not give her the edge of my tongue in my anger, but instead turned on my heels and slammed the door.

For days, there was a pall of mourning throughout the country.

I listened for hours to the radio reporting the progress of the funeral train from Georgia to Washington, then to the funeral service itself and the burial in Hyde Park. It was a season of great events and great tragedy. The war came to an end in Europe, and the atomic bomb was dropped on Hiroshima. This, too, was an event that you would remember until your dying day—where you were and what you were doing at the moment you heard the news.

So vivid was that memory that twenty-five years later, when I wrote an article for the *Boston Globe* on the anniversary of the dropping of the bomb, I had no problem recalling the profound emotions I had felt.

A 1945 Memory - And The Lesson

It was one of those deceptively soft, warm days in August in New Hampshire when it seemed that summer might go on forever in spite of the warning signs: wispy fog in the valley in the early morning, the sumac slightly reddened, and the rash of goldenrod already beginning to spread across the fields and along the stone walls. I can remember the feeling of the pine needles under my bare feet as I walked to the mail box, hoping for a letter from Europe. It had rained the night before and it was damp under the pines that lined the road. There was a smell of freshly washed leaves and grass in the air, which was utterly still, except for the hum of bumblebees in a patch of blackberry bushes. I remember it so vividly, I suppose, because it was the last time I would ever see or feel like that again for a long time if, indeed, ever again. For, in the *New York Herald Tribune*, in screaming headlines, was announced the dropping of the atomic bomb on Hiroshima.

One read it in dazzled, uncomprehending wonder at the magnitude of the scientific daring and accomplishment, in sickening horror at the enormity of the slaughter, and relief at the shortening of the agonizing war. And then, slowly, like the great expanding mushroom cloud of the bomb itself, one was flooded by the realization that one's life and everything one cared about on earth had changed irrevocably and forever.

In that searing flash, the past, the present, and the future were revealed as in a dream, and one knew that the world had been totally transformed. For in the hands of man were the tools of not only his own total destruction, but of all living things and matter as well as the planet itself. I can remember being overwhelmed by a sense of bottomless desolation, of incredible intensity and poignancy. With the dropping of the atomic bomb, history was rendered meaningless; all art and literature, all human learning, all that enhanced our lives, nature itself, were as dust and ashes. For history and human culture are premised on the simple, fundamental fact that man goes on living without fear of absolute extermination.

One realized in a single nightmarish moment how fragile were all the assumptions by which one lived—the inevitability of the seasons, the flight of birds in the spring, the turning of leaves in the autumn, even the blades of grass poking up between the cracks in a city sidewalk in the heat of summer, all the signs with which we mark off the days and years of our lives, and, above all, the presumption of perpetual life on earth no matter how we used and abused the gifts of nature. We took it for granted that life would go on forever. And now man and his institutions were exposed in all their vulnerability and mortality.

Suddenly we were no safer than a colony of ants under the shadow of a giant hobnailed boot which could crush and annihilate us at any moment. And like the ants, programmed by nature to go through certain unchanging motions, we too were pursuing the age-old patterns of human activity in the context of expectations which no longer existed. For the past had become irrelevant, human knowledge pointless, human striving ridiculous. The unknown is known, and all is desolation!

Such were the thoughts which overwhelmed my mind. We knew then that we were alive on sufferance. Those of us who experienced the first awful insight lived with it at the top of our consciousness for a long time. We were obsessed and could think of nothing else. But no one could exist at such an unbearable pitch and after a time we chose to muffle the fact in our day-to-day discourse, slowly papering it over, encapsulating it in some secret recess of our subconscious. People seldom speak of atomic holocaust today, but it is the basic fact of our age.

All the worn-out nineteenth-century shibboleths by which the nations of the world have been carrying on their mutual affairs of war and peace in these last decades seem ludicrous in the face of this appalling incubus. The old power alignments and the old power thinking are archaic when tomorrow we could blow the world to bits and in the process be blown to bits ourselves. No one ever wins in an atomic war.

Is this not the lesson and the opportunity of the late twentieth century? Is this not the moment for men to put away childish things, stop playing childish games and move beyond adolescence into adulthood? For truly mature people accept the truth that no one, in the larger sense, can indeed ever win. It does not mean that one is necessarily immobilized as a result. One is in fact freed by the knowledge. Perhaps we are being propelled willy-nilly by the horror of the atomic threat into a new adulthood and collective responsibility which nothing else in the history of this fated planet could have brought to bear. Perhaps, but the signs are not encouraging. If not, we will be just another burned-out star observed a billion light years from now in some unknown universe.

5

The Fifties

WE SPENT A YEAR AND A HALF in Washington after the war, enjoying a return to a more normal life. Arthur's book, *The Age of Jackson*, which he had completed before going abroad, was published in 1945 while he was still an Army corporal, stationed in Germany. The book became a best seller and won the Pulitzer Prize for history. Arthur began to write long pieces for national magazines like *Life* and *Fortune*. In an article for *Life* in 1946, he stirred up a storm by pointing out that the fellow-traveler mentality existed in parts of the labor movement, and he was maligned as provocatively anti-Communist at a time when relations with the USSR were still in a roseate state.

These were years of expanding friendships and horizons, living in a larger world than we had occupied as students and young instructors in the confines of academia. We were fortunate to move in an interesting circle, Democrats all, including Kay and Phil Graham, before they ran the *Washington Post*, erstwhile FDR special assistant Jim Rowe and his wife, lawyer Joe Rauh, paragon of energy and commitment to the causes of civil rights and civil liberties, and the two great wits, Ed Prichard and Isaiah Berlin, the first, the brilliant Kentucky protégé of Felix Frankfurter and assistant to Attorney General Francis Biddle, the second, the brilliant Oxonian, then attached to the British Embassy, who had been Prime Minister Churchill's favorite reporter on American affairs during the war. In his political activity, Arthur, along with liberal activists Rauh, James Wechsler (later editor of the *New York Post*), Jonathan Bingham (later congressman from New York), theologian and political thinker Rheinhold Niebuhr, and others, founded Americans for Democratic Action, to identify and promote liberal political policies.

Our second daughter, Christina, was born in Washington in 1946. I can remember sitting by her crib at my drawing board, having taken up my brush once again, doing the illustrations for the official coloring book of Colonial Williamsburg. Considering the fact that the publication sold for more than thirty years, I feel that I have been somewhat short-changed, having been paid a paltry $500. But at the time it seemed like riches.

With the end of the gasoline rationing, there were expeditions with the children to country fairs in little towns in the lovely Maryland countryside or down the river to Mount Vernon on the soft spring days so characteristic of Washington in April and May. How I loved the smell of box hedges in the gardens of Mount Vernon and the sweep of grass under the trees pouring down to the Potomac. The children and I agreed that George Washington really would have had to be a Hercules to throw a silver dollar across such a river.

Two of the Schlesinger children, Chrissie and Andy,
by MCS, 1955

Arthur was appointed an assistant professor at Harvard, to begin in the fall of 1947, so once again we said good-bye to our beautiful capital city and returned to "real life" in Cambridge. We bought a large Victorian house at 109 Irving Street, which had belonged to a professor of entomology at Harvard, who died at the age of 99, having built the house in 1893. I don't know if Professor Mark would have appreciated that I painted the dark oak woodwork white throughout the house and tore off the imitation, pressed Moroccan leather covering from the dining room walls, or that I used his meticulously maintained storage drawers in which he had kept his bug specimens to cache tubes of paint, brushes, pencils, pastels, as well as nails, screws, brads, screw drivers, hammers, chisels, rasps, and all the rest of the paraphernalia necessary to the functioning of a house.

As a result of the general chaos of the war, like so much of the rest of the world, Cambridge had changed. For so long a rather provincial academic community, it had begun to emerge into the great world, attracting a various and eclectic population and some unique institutions. With the founding of the Brattle Theatre Company in 1948 by a group of bright, young returning veterans, one could see in the space of a few weeks Chekhov's *Three Sisters*, a Pirandello or a Shakespeare, or Eugene O'Neill's *Moon for the Misbegotten*, wonderfully acted on the Brattle's creaky wooden stage. Many of the company's gifted actors, including Zero Mostel, Jessica Tandy, and Hume Cronyn, went on to distinguished careers on Broadway and in Hollywood.

The Window Shop, almost next door to the Brattle, was on the site of the Old Village Blacksmith's shop. It was a unique institution, organized by prominent Cambridge women, formed to give employment and financial aid to the streams of German Jews and other displaced intellectuals escaping from Nazi Germany. The Window Shop became a fixture in Harvard Square, selling Viennese pastries and dresses, that forever transformed the diet of Cantabridgians with a rich flow of apfelstrudels and linzertortes and turned out two or three generations of dirndl-garbed girls, and rather disastrously, two or three generations of dirndl-garbed middle-aged ladies.

The influx of so many of these German and middle European refugees had a profound impact on the community. The fifties became the decade in which a whole generation of young architects were influenced by the teaching of Walter Gropius, a Bauhaus veteran and professor at the Harvard Graduate School of Design. Gropius established the Architects Collaborative which executed important commissions around the country and abroad. Dr. Helene Deutsch, the distinguished Viennese psychoanalyst and protégée of Freud, who had found a haven in Cambridge after her flight from Hitler in 1935, helped make Cambridge and Boston a significant center for psychoanalysis. As with the Bauhaus architects, the Viennese psychoanalysts imported their aesthetic as well. The interior decor of their offices was so typical: steel-gray, wall-to-wall carpeting, steel-gray walls on which hung Käthe Kollwitz lithographs and pseudo-Kokoshka paintings, and on the desk a relic or two or an antique statuette.

Even the Cambridge of my childhood was changing and disappearing. Having grown up on nearby Divinity Avenue, I was somewhat shocked to discover the lawns around the buildings of the Divinity School covered with Nissen huts housing returning graduate students, many attending Harvard on the G.I. Bill, and their families. The aging neighborhood was thronged with children, and as the ancients died out, we acquired a new set of neighbors. Rabbi Maurice Zigmond and his family lived across the street in the Hillel House, and, over the brick wall, the Galbraith ménage with the towering figure of Ken became a community landmark.

The first party we gave on our return to Cambridge was on the night of Truman's reelection on November 2, 1948. It turned out to be God's gift to the hostess. We gathered friends to listen to the returns and mourn Truman's inevitable demise, but as the evening wore on our excitement grew. Favorable returns began to mount. By early morning the wake had turned into a gala, as the corpse came to life, and the party was the success of the season. I listened to Dewey's concession speech on the car radio the next day as I drove into Boston for a doctor's appointment. I always remember the date of my younger son's birth, two weeks to the day after that fateful night.

Each morning, having dispatched the twins to the Agassiz school, the same local school I had attended as a child, having delivered Christina to nursery school and consigned baby Andrew to the tender mercies of a sweet high school girl, I returned to the important business of painting portraits and participating in local politics. Arthur was anchored in his study, writing the first of his books on the presidency of Franklin D. Roosevelt. I remember his technique as a baby sitter, once placing Christina in a large wastepaper basket beside his desk, where she happily spent a good hour tearing up discarded pieces of paper and dropping them in a pile at his feet, while he typed away, amazingly oblivious and unperturbed by the general noise and confusion of a large household of children, relatives and friends roiling about him.

My baptism into political campaigning had begun at an early age. As an inveterate campaigner for social uplift through the "political process," my mother was a great one for ringing doorbells and canvassing for reform candidates in Cambridge back in the dim days of the 1920s when Mayor Quinn and "The Boys from City Hall" presided over the city. She used to take me along, to stumble up dark, unlit wooden staircases in boarding houses and three deckers in the back streets behind Central Square or in East Cambridge. She solicited signatures from startled inhabitants: blowzy landladies in felt slippers and curl papers, weary shirt-sleeved laborers, and incoherent drunks, who could hardly hold a pencil and who certainly were not in favor of her candidate. I remember the smells, sour and depressing, and the autumn chill in the late afternoon when it was dark by five o'clock. But no matter how cold my unmittened hands and no matter how often I wished myself home safe and sound, I suppose these expeditions inculcated some sense of civic responsibility that had a lasting effect. The amazing thing is that they didn't alienate me from politics forever.

There was always a good deal of discussion around the house about the evils of the incumbents and the inevitability of their reelection. In a letter to her mother in St. Paul, my mother summed up her philosophical view of her political efforts after another electoral disappointment: "I have taken up my civic responsibilities once again. I have been busy getting signatures to nomination papers, women out to register, and all the rest of the labor to get a democracy to run your way. And how entirely it runs the other way!" No matter how despondent, she rose like the Phoenix to take up her civic duties once again, like so many Cambridge women before and since.

With time, I, too, took up the political cudgels. Full of

enthusiasm and optimism, we were determined to bring civic reform to Cambridge. Back then, before today's peripatetic times, people were apt to stay put. The same names at the same addresses appeared year after year on the voting list, and we learned who could be depended on to vote "our" way or who would be willing to canvass their block or apartment building. We threw ourselves into the battle, becoming an eager corps of bell-ringers and telephoners, scanning lists of possible "yes" voters, and seeing that they got to the polls on Election Day.

The 1940s and '50s were comparatively innocent days. We felt that as individuals we could make a difference. "We" meant liberal-minded, action-oriented, middle-class women, either at home taking care of children or working in a variety of jobs and professions. We shared a desire to be out in the world, participating in the political process. We were less interested in national politics than in the problems of our local communities. Washington seemed far away, and the national Democratic Party, which claimed the loyalty of many of us, appeared to be bumbling along without our help. Anyway, in the state of Massachusetts, the Democratic machine did not seem very interested in our participation. Its attitude was a parochial one—a woman's place is in the home, so forget it!

It took the candidacy of Adlai Stevenson for the presidency on the Democratic ticket in 1952 to bring many of us women into the arena of national politics. To be sure, there had been a major effort to organize women for political action during the first two terms of the Roosevelt Administration under the leadership of Eleanor Roosevelt, and it had succeeded in developing a network

Marian with Adlai Stevenson, 1956

of women workers throughout the country. But with the distraction of the war and the particular character of the Truman administration, much of the impulse had dissipated, so Stevenson's nomination was a spark, firing up the women's movement

For some reason, I had not been particularly aware of Stevenson or who he was—the governor of Illinois or something like that. During the summer of 1952, I had taken the children to visit my sister in northern Minnesota and then flown down to Chicago to join Arthur at the Democratic National Convention, where he was working for Averell Harriman. It was only then that I became transported by the Stevenson phenomenon. I can remember with what mounting excitement I watched from the balcony of the International Amphitheatre the voting of the delegates and the roar as Stevenson was victorious on the third ballot. I had heard plenty of political speeches over the radio and attended a huge, enthusiastic rally for Roosevelt in the Boston Garden in October 1940. But this was something different. When Stevenson finally appeared and delivered his acceptance speech, the atmosphere was wildly euphoric. A new star was born. A man of irresistible wit, eloquence, and spirit had arrived to enrich and enliven the political scene and inspire a whole generation of young people. Like so many others, I was hooked.

Arthur and I returned to Minnesota to pick up the children. We were about to start on the long drive back to Cambridge when Stevenson called Arthur and invited him to join the campaign. And so, instead, we drove to Springfield, skirting the Mississippi much of the way, in a state of high spirits in spite of sweltering heat in which, as the saying goes, you could hear the corn growing. I remember the small towns through which we drove with their neat white churches and small wooden houses set well back from the elm-shaded streets, with people swinging on their porch hammocks or sitting on the front steps, cooling off after the heat of the day. I recall being moved by the sight of one of the little river towns, Prairie du Chien, Wisconsin, where my father had been born.

We arrived in Springfield at the Executive Mansion late on the second afternoon. The inside of the car resembled a compost pit. The children were knee-deep in candy wrappers, torn comic books, coke bottles, orange peels, and melting Dairy Queens

Two delightful young men, Carl McGowan and Bill Blair, aides to Governor Stevenson, took us in hand, unfazed by a scruffy family of six. And when Stevenson himself emerged from the Mansion to welcome us, I almost fainted, seeing my hero in the flesh. He very sweetly took our elder son into his office to show him a letter written by Abraham Lincoln, framed on his office wall. The next evening we were all asked to dinner in the garden of the Mansion where the only discordant note was struck when Mrs. Ives, Stevenson's sister and hostess, placed the children at a table with only corn flakes for dinner while the rest of us dined on delicious cold salmon and asparagus tips. I always thought that our youngest, Andrew, three-and-a-half, expressed some sort of editorial complaint by falling into the fishpond.

I went back to Cambridge with the children while Arthur stayed on in Springfield. With two other women, old hands at working in local politics, we organized the Stevenson headquarters in an empty store in Harvard Square where we were overrun with volunteers: housewives with two-year-olds in tow, students, professional men and women dropping in after work, secretaries on their lunch hours, stamp lickers, telephoners, money raisers, doorbell ringers, literature dispensers, and envelope addressers. They swarmed over us like a battalion of ants. In fact, it became a paradigm of every political campaign I was ever involved in afterwards, and no doubt the best. Though winning would have made it even better.

In 1952, Jack Kennedy was running for the U.S. Senate against Henry Cabot Lodge Jr., but there was little connection between the Kennedy and Stevenson campaigns. This was characteristic of the divisions within the state Democratic Party. There was a good deal of suspicion—even hostility—from the established politicians toward the enthusiastic neophytes and so-called "do-gooders," whom the professionals saw as a threat. On the other hand, the Kennedys always ran their own campaigns close to the chest, with no thanks to any other group that might try to horn in.

Many years later, I remember Bobby Kennedy sitting at my right hand at dinner at our house in Washington in the early days of the Kennedy Administration. I had not met him before that evening, and without further ado, he turned to me and asked, in a rather belligerent tone, "Were you for Jack in 1952?" Then he added, with something of a sneer, "Or were you for Stevenson?" Since they weren't running for the same office, I thought the question rather strange, and I felt befuddled. I mumbled something to the effect that, "Of course, I was for Jack, but I was working primarily for Stevenson," and let it go at that, hoping he would stop boring in on me. It was only later that I recalled that our efforts during the Stevenson campaign to combine forces with the Kennedys had met with sharp rebuffs. The Kennedy campaign had obviously wanted no part of the Stevenson effort, looking on it as pure poison as far as Jack's run for the Senate. As for Bobby Kennedy's remarks to me, I now reflect that he may have been teasing, though in a very heavy-handed way, for we became good friends.

So it was not the Kennedy campaign in 1952 that electrified so many of my contemporaries. It was the witty, eloquent person of Adlai Stevenson who spoke to us as no other political figure had since Roosevelt, as we threw ourselves with demonic energy into Stevenson's run for the presidency. We were able to put all the volunteers to work because of our past experience in local politics. We knew a good deal about the city, where to turn and how to go about organizing. In fact, we ran such an efficient headquarters that a few egregious Harvard Law students tried to take over the operation, no doubt feeling that their macho presence would add the necessary authority and that we women, who had gotten things started, could now turn it over to the pros. They were told to DROP DEAD!

Apropos of this and later experiences in politics, I have reflected how typical it was that women so often did most of the dirty work. It may not be as true today, though I doubt it. So-called policy-making (that is, political activity without pain) seems to have been an exclusive male preserve, involving rich, bibulous lunches, high-level steak dinners, expense accounts, and a good deal of superfluous yak. It seems to me that most political decisions involve basic premises that any sensible person, male or female, can come up with, even without props, gustatorial or otherwise. The hard labor of the ward and precinct denizens, getting voters to the polls for instance, so often performed by women, really wins elections.

The psychology of a campaign is certainly curious. I found myself willing to call up perfect strangers, whom I would not consider approaching otherwise, and asking them for large donations of money, especially money for television advertising in the last hectic days of the campaign. Unrealistic hopes are another phenomenon of political campaigns, and we were borne along by such hopes throughout the October weeks of 1952. It was not until Eisenhower drove through Harvard Square in his motorcade and was ecstatically mobbed not only by the citizenry of Cambridge but by blasé Harvard students that we knew we were in real trouble.

Late in October I traveled on the Stevenson train on a whistle-stop tour of Southern New England. I remember that the candidate spoke to excited crowds in Providence and New Haven and that the train was running late that evening between New Haven and New York. The cars were thronged with newspapermen. The noise and squawk of radios was deafening. The cigarette smoke was almost impenetrable. It was the height of the Joe McCarthy madness, and the Wisconsin senator was giving a radio speech, which was broadcast throughout the train. To my utter surprise, McCarthy suddenly started attacking my husband, Arthur, my brother-in-law, the Chinese expert John K. Fairbank, and our friend Bernard DeVoto, author and speechwriter, as dyed-in-the-wool Reds and Communists. With his reckless accusations, McCarthy had already destroyed the lives of many innocent men and woman. I wondered fearfully when he would discover that I had worked as a lowly researcher for the Institute for Pacific Relations in New York in the 1930s, an organization that was one of his favorite targets. That train ride was a peculiar experience, unreal and eerie, even scary. There was a feeling of dread in the air.

My hairdresser, a streetwise Delphic oracle, pointed out that the best way to measure the political pulse was to follow the presidential straw votes taken in public high schools throughout the state. And she was right. They were overwhelmingly for Ike. And so another political chapter came to an end, though we succeeded in carrying Cambridge for Stevenson by a goodly margin. We would fight for him again, in 1956, but in our heart of hearts we knew it was hopeless. The 1950s was the age of Eisenhower, and nothing and no one could alter it.

Yet the sinister shenanigans of Senator Joe McCarthy continued at full tilt even after Ike's inauguration. McCarthy had turned the anti-Communist hysteria of the time to his own political purposes, smearing his enemies as fellow travelers, party members, even Soviet spies. But he eventually went too far, becoming embroiled with Eisenhower's Secretary of the Army and revealing himself as a mendacious bully when hearings were broadcast on national television.

We were mesmerized by the Army-McCarthy hearings in 1954. We had one of the first televisions in the neighborhood, and I think we were considered rather vulgar by some of our high-minded neighbors, corrupters of young minds. But it was interesting that a goodly number of them dropped by to view the brouhaha. The children may have gotten a good civics lesson, but their chief reaction was irritation when they came home from school for lunch and there was nothing to eat. The cooks were too glued to the television! Needless to say, Arthur sat through it all imperturbably, typing away even though the TV was planted in his study and the throng of children and adults surged about. His only complaint was a reaction to the children's quarreling about who got to sit on the couch. "Marian, take the children away," he cried. "They're behaving worse than McCarthy!"

The 1950s unwound slowly. The children grew older. Arthur brought out three volumes of his series on the years of President Franklin Roosevelt. I painted portraits in my third-floor studio at one end of the children's playroom, with their piles of blocks and electric trains at the other. A parade of kindly, sweet-natured, Irish cleaning ladies came and went. I especially remember Delia, the keening Delia, the ravaged, beautiful Delia, who with her soft heartbreaking brogue used to reduce me to tears with her tales of family tragedies in Ireland and her poignant longing for her lost homeland. To be sure, she almost blew up the house when she forgot to light the gas oven, with Christina sitting in her high chair right beside it. Finally, Delia disappeared, some disaster having overtaken her, I fear. Many years later, on reading a life of Nora, the wife of James Joyce, I felt I recognized her type. She reminded me of Delia. With this new insight, I even felt I might try reading *Ulysses* again, now that I had some idea of what it was all about from reading Nora's biography. I have come across many "Noras" in my lifetime in Cambridge, but never one more closely akin than Delia with her passionate love of her country and her capacity to move me to tears.

All was not necessarily politics. Culture was in the air. The ladies of Cambridge flocked to hear Isaiah Berlin's lectures on Russian nineteenth-century intellectual history, and I was among the flockers. Isaiah stood before the adoring audience, looking neither right nor left but at some distant corner of the lecture room, high above the heads of the ladies and of the throng of undergraduates, and delivered his lecture at such pistol speed that it took all of one's concentration to follow his words. He confided in me that he was afraid to look at his audience for fear of being undone by their uncomprehending faces. The lectures were fascinating and sent me off to read about the Decembrists and other political radicals. There was a run on the novels of Turgenev, Tolstoy, and Dostoyevsky at the Coop and for the nonce the ladies were deep in Russian culture.

Scholars doing research in the various Harvard libraries and museums came and went, many of them residing in our academic enclave. Among the more exotic roomers staying with one of the neighbors was Jean van Heijenoort, who had served as a secretary and bodyguard for Leon Trotsky in Mexico City and was unfortunately absent the day Trotsky was murdered in 1940. Heijenoort worked on the Trotsky papers in the Houghton Library for some years, then went back to Mexico to rejoin his fourth wife, a Mexican woman from a distinguished family, who proceeded to murder him in a jealous rage in 1986. He must have been sexually irresistible as he was married four times and had an affair with Frida Kahlo, Diego Rivera's wife, apparently among others. Who knows what wreckage he may have left behind in Cambridge, Massacusetts?

Those were the days when Cambridge hostesses with their maids and cooks still prevailed. And a few of them presided over cultural salons of a kind. Among them was our neighbor at 95 Irving Street, Mrs. William James, the daughter-in-law of the philosopher William James. She was a large and imperious opéra-bouffe character, faintly malaproprian, who was given to finishing the sentences of her rather shy husband, the painter and portraitist. Billy was a slow starter, finding enunciation of his ideas a painful process, and Alice would sweep down upon him telling him in no uncertain terms what he wished to say. He sweetly deferred to her, never raising any protest. She concentrated on literary types, preferably the English, entertaining W.H. Auden and Stephen Spender when they came to speak or read their poems in the New Lecture Hall, or Osbert and Edith Sitwell (she swathed in stiff maroon brocade) when they performed before an ecstatic audience in Sanders Theatre.

A friend of mine was once called up on the day of one of her parties by Alice James (all James females seem to be named Alice), who explained, "We were going to have a small party, a very small party, for Isaiah Berlin. But the list gets bigger and bigger. So we decided to have everybody, just everybody! Won't you come?" My friend was too enchanted to refuse.

A steady stream of interesting people flowed in and out of our house on Irving Street, many new acquaintances made through Arthur's political activities. We had a "celebratory" party for Stevenson after his 1952 defeat at which Tom Lehrer, that master of black humor, sang his brilliant, satirical songs and Adlai's ardent followers gathered to wish him well. Danny Kaye and his wife, Sylvia Fine, an interesting pair, came for drinks. I remember that I took Sylvia to see the glass flowers at the Agassiz Museum at her request. It amused me to accompany her. As a child, I had been bidden by my mother to take foreign students of my father's to "see the glass flowers," a sign that the conversation in broken German or French had ground to a halt and something had to be done to "entertain" the young men.

The 1950s seemed to be the decade of the English. Barbara

Ward, the handsome blue-stocking economist and Africanist, took the economics department by storm. We had her to dinner numerous times and often at her royal command, supplying us with her own guest list. The children finally complained that they were sick of hearing about the imports and exports of Ghana, and I rather sympathized, but I was actually sicker about the dirty dishes that resulted. Along with her obvious intellectual brilliance that had the likes of Adlai Stevenson and John F. Kennedy swooning, Barbara was a typical English sponge, who got out of town before she might feel any urge to return the favor. Not that it really mattered, but a gesture would have been welcome.

During the excitement of the Kennedy presidential run, the English writer John Strachey came to stay for two or three nights, an overflow from the Galbraith ménage. I would not have minded, but Arthur was out of town and I was left to "entertain" a rather taciturn and difficult man who obviously thought I was just another tiresome woman; and no eggcup in the morning! He made his getaway with hardly a nod. Arthur Koestler was another moody but interesting overnight guest, who was fascinated by the fact that my father was the author of *Bodily Changes in Pain, Hunger, Fear and Rage*, based on his studies of the effects of emotions on the body. My father's work had led to the development of psychosomatic medicine, a concept in which Koestler was apparently deeply interested. Arthur remembers taking a copy of *Darkness at Noon* down from the shelves to be autographed and discovering that it had "W.B. Cannon" inscribed inside, with annotations and underlinings throughout the text.

Koestler was pleased and asked whether he could have the book, promising to send another copy in exchange. As Arthur recalls, he did not have the heart to tell him that the penciling was all in his mother-in-law's handwriting.

Most amusing to me was another British guest, Malcolm Muggeridge, a mordant wit who went on to become editor of *Punch* and then a star of British and American television, memorable for his outrageous pronouncements. Sitting over breakfast one morning, I remember his making me laugh when he asked, "Do you know why Trappist monks are called Trappists? Because they keep their traps shut." An old gag and simple-minded but it seemed funny at the time when spoken in his sepulchral voice.

Several British politicians came for dinner, like Roy Jenkins, already a distinguished historian and MP, and David Ormsby-Gore, later Lord Harlech and British Ambassador in Washington during the Kennedy Administration. And so the British came and went, and with many we enjoyed their company.

Then there were our good friends Myron and Sheila Gilmore who lived at the end of Divinity Avenue in an old wooden nine-teenth-century house later moved to make way for the biology labs. Myron was professor of medieval history and chairman of the history department, and Sheila, a real original, was in a way my alter ego. We shared the same sardonic take on the passing scene and held strong opinions on everything—politics, colleagues, friends and neighbors, academia in general, the state of the world. A lot of good gossip flavored our daily telephone calls. Sheila was the step-granddaughter of Alfred North Whitehead, the distinguished English philosopher lured away from Oxford to join the Harvard faculty. He had arrived in Cambridge with his extended family including not only his elegant aristocratic wife and his daughter Jessie (best known around Cambridge for riding her bicycle through Harvard Square with a colorful parakeet on each shoulder), but also seventeen-year-old Sheila, a messy English school girl set down in the midst of Cambridge to sink or swim.

Like so many English upper-class children, Sheila had been sent off to boarding school as a little girl of eight (something that would be considered child abuse in the present day mores of child-rearing in this country), a staunch little figure who claimed that she enjoyed every minute of her boarding school days. It was in a way a metaphor for the rest of her life, a facing of facts and the realities of existence with courage, humor, and fun, her ironic eye cast at so many absurdities of the passing scene. At last she swam, grew up, and married Myron Gilmore, at that point a promising graduate student in history and literature. Then, after her four children had been launched into various academies and high schools, she found time on her hands. What to do? She reflected that she was no scholar, did not know how to type, and had no talent for good works, but she knew one thing. She was a good cook. So when her friend, Charles Merrill, head of Boston's Commonwealth School, complained at some cocktail party that he was having a hard time finding a cook for the school, she announced, "How about me?"

Thus began eight years of inspired lunches for the children of the Commonwealth School. Glorious pastas, tasty paella, and savory soups provided a subtle lesson in geography as well as a stimulus to the taste buds. This was many years before cooking became the fashion among the well heeled, and there were raised eyebrows among some of her friends who preferred to refer to her role, if they referred to it at all, as chef. It seemed somehow more genteel. But her children who were at the stage where they had to fill out applications for boarding schools or colleges took delight in writing: Father—Chairman, History Department, Harvard University; Mother—Cook.

Until Benny's death in 1955, Arthur and I often went for cocktails on Sunday afternoons at the DeVotos' great Victorian house with its magnificent library on Berkeley Street. Benny was a historian of the American West and a passionate conservationist who wrote an influential column for *Harper's Magazine* in which he tirelessly called for preservation of the country's natural resources. Avis was a wonderfully active, high-spirited character with a voice full of pep and verve who was later instrumental in getting Julia Child's famous cookbook published. Their guests were a mixed bag: literary types, academics, visiting writers, and a psychoanalyst or two, as Benny was fascinated by psychoanalysis. So the talk consisted of an amalgam of literary gossip, academic backbiting, and psychoanalytic chat. Benny mixed the martinis according to an inflexible formula of his own creation, which he immortalized in a little book entitled *The Hour: A Cocktail Manifesto*, considered by many to be an essential volume.

Another occasion from that period stays in my mind. We were asked to dinner by Henry Kissinger, at that time an aspiring young instructor in the government department, and his nice first wife in their suburban house in Belmont. The food was heavy, the talk was ponderous and male, the ladies were silent, and after dinner the gentlemen sat at one end of the living room and the ladies at the other. I recall thinking that if ever there was an example of a heavy-footed "Herr Professor," Henry Kissinger was it. Who would have guessed that he would turn out to be such a swinger? One wonders after all these years whether he is perhaps at heart still the heavy-footed Herr Professor.

And I must not forget that raffish, one-legged wild man, Al Capp, creator of the comic strip *Li'l Abner*, who with his dear gentle wife Catherine came to live among us on Brattle Street. His presence struck a fresh note in the community as he brought a whiff of the N.Y. deli world to provincial Cambridge, as well as adding something new to the brew of types that were altering the scene. I never knew whether Catherine had a clue as to whom she had married or what he was up to. It probably wouldn't have stood too close an examination.

In the summers, we spent a month in Wellfleet, on Cape Cod, first in a delightfully primitive shack on a high sand cliff, over-looking the great outside beach, with nothing between us and the coast of Europe but the great heaving Atlantic Ocean. One woke early to see the gorgeous, uncluttered rise of the sun and then slide down the dunes and take a first dip in the sea, the beach empty as far as the eye could see. Housekeeping was nil, merely a swish of the broom to sweep the sand out the door, and we often dined on mussels culled by the children at the mouth of the Pamet River in Truro. Mussels were free for the taking in those days. The beach was a gathering place for the various denizens of the woods and the ponds, novelist Mary McCarthy and her husband, Bowden Broadwater, Harry and Elena Levin, Alfred Kazin and his wife Anne, Edmund and Elena Wilson, and especially Ed O'Connor, author of *The Last Hurrah.*

When we first knew Ed, his only form of transportation was his bicycle, on which he peddled himself to the beach from his boarding house in town, always laden with four or five books and dressed in his ragged, old bathing trunks and prehistoric leather sandals. He was a merry man, a droll man, and a magnet on the beach. Children adored him. Coming over the crest of the dunes, one swept the sand with one's eye to find where "Big Ed," as the children called him, had planted himself, his ancient terry cloth jacket jammed under his head as a pillow. He loved the big rolling surf as it came off the Atlantic and the heat of the sand, after the champagne-like sensation of the cool and brilliant water. He could idle away hours lying in the sun, reading and chatting, until you wondered how he ever got around to writing his books. He had in fact arisen at five in the morning and worked at least four solid hours before meandering, as though without a care in the world, to the ocean.

There was never a man whose good fortune and success gave his friends more pleasure. He was incapable of arousing emotions of envy and jealousy. People loved the fact that *The Last Hurrah* was a great best seller and made Ed some money. He always referred to the book as "Hurrah," as though it were embodied in some way and had a life of its own. With his royalties, he built a wonderful modern house, designed by another denizen of the

Ed O'Connor, c. 1960

woods, Serge Chermayeff. Arthur tried to get Ed together with President Kennedy, but Ed, a good Catholic, rather disapproved of Kennedy's lifestyle (I guess) and the meeting never took place. I am sure the President would have found him a delight, as all his friends did. But there is nothing like an Irishman against an Irishman when it comes down to it. Ed turned in his bicycle for a Porsche and married his lovely wife, Veniette, and died too soon, at age 49 in 1968.

As time went on, we acquired another delightful shack on Slough Pond, a five-minute walk from the beach on a sandy path skirted by beach plum bushes and low-growing wild cranberries and permeated in the early summer by the intoxicating fragrance of pink wild roses. Another sort of sunrise took place on our peaceful pond, the rays of the sun filtering through the branches of gnarled pines, so Japanese in feeling. The only sounds were the intermittent calls of the quail, which rustled through the underbrush, and the almost noiseless splash of the Chermayeffs, our neighbors, and their two German shepherd dogs, as they took their morning swim across the pond. Such peace! But not for long. For when Serge got back to his deck, the stentorian roar of his commands to his dogs and his perpetual demands and complaints to his wife, Barbara, carried undiminished across the water.

Serge used to complain bitterly about the noise our children made, perhaps justifiably. Some years later, I met him at a cocktail party and had the pleasure of teasing him, saying, "Really, Serge, your yelling at your dogs and your grandchildren is beginning to hurt my ears." He was the lord of the pond and a passionate environmentalist and conservationist. One was grateful for his sensitive ears when he banished an obtrusive motorboat, offensive to the spirit of the pond, by the furious outrage of his remarks and personality. The poor owner could not stand up against it and retired his motorboat for good.

We shared a party-line telephone with the Chermayeffs, and there was a certain amount of complaint when Arthur served in the Kennedy Administration and tied up the line with talks to the White House. It may have seemed exotic to begin with, but after a while it became a pain in the neck to the Chermayeffs. We finally broke down and got a private line

Arthur Schlesinger on the party line in Wellfleet, 1961

The woods were full of psychiatrists, writers, artists, atomic physicists, and especially architects, among them Marcel Breuer and Serge Chermayeff. Knowing them and their houses was for me an artistic education. For the first time, I saw the use of decks as outside auxiliary rooms, built of redwood, which through the years attained a wonderful dark patina. Decks have now become standard additions to many American houses, but in the 1950s they were a rarity, at least in the East. The interiors of their houses were simple and uncluttered, a single sling chair or director's chair in beige or oat-meal colored canvas, tatami on the floors, and, in the case of Breuer, a beautifully designed wooden couch, of which I took note and built a copy years later for myself. It was a lesson in "less is more."

As Edmund Wilson grew too old to huff and puff over the dunes to the beach, he frequently came by and dipped in our pond, arriving with his dear wife Elena, an aristocratic figure often dressed in a brilliant blue shift, which matched her glorious blue eyes. Edmund would wade into the water up to his knees in oversized bathing trunks ballooning out and a droopy pork-pie hat, crooning to his dog Brown. His relationship with his dog seemed to me his most profound relationship. In spite of his descriptions of his sexual escapades in such explicit detail in his published journals, it is difficult to think of Edmund as an irresistible sex object with his roly-poly figure and little, skinny, white, etiolated legs and pudgy, white hands. I still find it hard to understand that a man of such intellectual sophistication could behave so like an oversexed high school boy, necking with the Madame Bovarys of Talcottville, N.Y., all described in excruciating detail in his 1960s journal. And he in his advanced seventies!

Perhaps the reason Edmund wrote with such zest about his essays into fornication was because he wrote about all his other varied and eclectic interests with such enthusiasm. He was interested in everything from the Iroquois of Northern New York to the Dead Sea Scrolls. It is such a pleasure to read his journals and his volumes of criticism, so full of insights and shrewd and subtle perceptions and humanity (for some), intriguing descriptions of the parade of friends and characters who crossed his path.

To get back to the pond! Elena would sit with me on the deck and very kindly let me play chess with her. I was always making the worst possible moves, but she was generous and indulgent. She was a passionate Democrat (an interesting phenomenon in a member of the Mumm champagne family) and a great reader. Some years after Edmund's death, I remember her writing to me about my book *Snatched From Oblivion*, saying she was sure "Edmund would have loved it and would have wanted to write something about it." Too bad he wasn't still around, I thought.

Going to dinner at the Wilsons' was always interesting. After Elena had produced some succulent meal, Edmund would play the part of the *paterfamilias* as he carved the roast and served the vegetables, the only domestic chores I feel sure he ever performed. The charming living room in their little nineteenth-century sea-captain's house near the center of the village was white, white, white, with orange and yellow nasturtiums in a pretty glass bowl the only touch of color, beside a blue-and-white patch-work quilt that hung behind the couch.

Edmund was actually a charming host, always asking after your comfort and then yelling out to Elena to bring this or that. He loved to play solitaire on the table in front of the couch, but his conversation more often than not consisted of monologues. If by chance someone tossed up a subject, Edmund might run with it. Or, if he was not interested, he would just as easily say, "I don't want to talk about that!" He was not one to make concessions or waste time with other people's interests if they did not interest him. Yet he could do such disarming things. He once planted

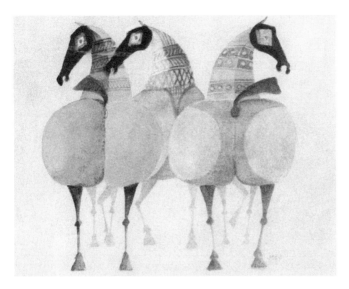

Horses *by MCS, c. 1961*

a mechanical butterfly in a book in Widener Library and then wrote Arthur suggesting a quote that might interest him in the same book on the same page where the butterfly was planted. When the book opened to that page, the butterfly flew up into Arthur's face! Edmund was a clever "magician" and prestidigitator and did amusing shows for the children in Wellfleet, often in collaboration with Ed O'Connor, a rare team indeed.

Edmund was very appreciative of my paintings and bought two, which I think still hang in the house in Wellfleet. And he paid me the ultimate compliment by asking me to draw one of my stylized horses with his diamond-tipped stylus on a windowpane in the house. I think I was in good company, Pavel Tchelitchew and Auden among others having left their marks. We both shared a liking for Edward Lear's drawings, not only his witty illustrations for his book of limericks, but his wonderful architectural and landscape watercolors and wash drawings of Rome, Southern Italy, Greece and the Levant. And knowing my interest in Lear and in India, Edmund thoughtfully gave me a book from his library, a copy of Lear's account of his expedition to India in the 1880s, full of enchanting illustrations of oxen, elephants, palmy shores, Hindu temples, and Rajput palaces. I treasure it.

— 6 —

JFK Comes to Irving Street

No doubt, through the years, many famous and interesting people had been in and out of the living rooms of the houses along Irving Street, but I wonder whether any included a President-elect of the United States. It was in the long living room of our house one January afternoon in 1961 that Jack Kennedy chose some of the men who went with him to Washington. He had asked Arthur if he could use our house, while in town attending a meeting of the Harvard Overseers, for interviewing prospective members of his administration. It was a bitter, leaden-gray day with no snow, but the threat hung heavily in the air. I remember that McGeorge Bundy, then the dean of the faculty, arrived on his bicycle and parked it in the front yard where, for once, it was safe from pilferers as there seemed to be a whole battalion of Cambridge cops guarding the house. The Secret Service had come the day before and spread out through the rooms, examining entrances and exits. They had reconnoitered the backyard and asked questions about the neighbors, one a bed-ridden old lady, another a timid paleontologist, and the third, looming over the garden wall, John Kenneth Galbraith at six-foot-nine inches.

That morning, the Cambridge police put up sawhorses along Irving Street, and by mid-afternoon five or six policemen patrolled the street, flailing their arms to keep warm in the frigid weather. The fallen leaves scudded along, driven by the wind, making scratchy noises against the front steps and the granite curbstones. The neighbors began to gather until the street outside, usually so deserted, was full of children on bicycles and mothers with their babies in carriages, bundled against the cold. Even the usually blasé graduate students stopped on their well trodden paths to gape, and interlopers came together in knots leaning against the Tozzers' brick wall across the street. The only dissenting voice appeared to be an elderly neighbor, a staunch Republican, who complained, when she had to alight from her chauffeur-driven car and walk a half a block to her house, "all because some Irishman has been elected president."

Many years later I had a charming experience. I had attended an interesting occasion at the local grammar school, which I had attended as a child, the Agassiz School. It was being renamed the Baldwin School in honor of Maria Baldwin who back in the 1920s had been the first and only black principal of a public school in Massachusetts (and a woman at that!). The occasion was presided over by the present principal, an attractive Irish woman who told me the following story. She had been a 12-year-old schoolgirl in North Cambridge back in 1961 and, like so many other schoolgirls, besotted with John F. Kennedy.

JFK on front steps of 109 Irving Sreet, early January 1961
Courtesy of *The Boston Globe*

When she read in the papers that JFK was coming to our house on Irving Street, she and another girl had skipped school and come to stand across the street to look adoringly at their hero as he came and went in and out of the house. I hope she had a good view of him.

The excitement was electric when the parade of black Cadillacs drew up and the President-elect emerged from one limousine, trailed by newspaper photographers, Secret Service men, and various nameless aides. Without missing a step, he turned and waved to the crowd, then shook hands with the cops whose beaming faces seemed to bespeak their inner thoughts, "Here's one of ours." Kennedy quickly bounded up the steps, so vigorous, so vital, so attractive. Inside, he shook hands with members of the household shyly lined up in awe to greet him, various children and their lucky best pals, and two sweet Irish cleaning women, angels of order, who took turns resolving the chaos of a hectic household. Then he disappeared into the living room.

At one point, Kennedy had to use a private telephone. I recall his vaulting up the staircase, two steps at a time, to use the phone in my catchall of a "sewing room," where I had thrown all the general refuse of the family—shoes, toys, discarded children's clothes, cancelled checks on my desk, and no doubt children's half-eaten, peanut-butter-and-jelly sandwiches—thinking that no one would penetrate the room, much less a future president of the United States. It was in the midst of this mess that he no doubt conducted high-level government business, or, according to later testimony, perhaps other and less exalted affairs of state. At any rate, the telephone was hardly "secure." No matter how rueful I felt to be "found out," I am sure he could not have cared less.

I first met Jack Kennedy when he came to our house for Sunday lunch in the early spring of 1952. He was then the U.S. Representative for the Massachusetts 10th District. He was delivered at the door by one of his hirelings, who sat hunched behind the wheel of a black Olds for at least two hours in the chilly April cold. There seemed always to be small, goony creatures in large black cars waiting for Kennedys outside houses, restaurants or meeting halls, no matter how cold the weather or how long the stay. The other guests were the McGeorge Bundys and Paul Douglas, U.S. Senator from Illinois, who was in Cambridge to deliver the Godkin Lectures at Harvard. A rigorous Spartan and an incorruptibly honest man, Douglas in one lecture supported the unenforceable thesis that no elected official should accept a gift worth more than $10. Even then, $10 was not much, and I expect his proposal would have been greeted by hoots from the rest of the Senate.

At lunch there was some discussion of Kennedy's running for the Senate in the fall. In much the same spirit of rigorous rectitude expressed in his lectures, Douglas rather patronizingly advised the young man that it would be better to serve his apprenticeship in the House for a few more terms before moving on. I was intrigued by Kennedy's response. His manners could not have been more respectful, as he listened to his elders and putative betters with what appeared to be thoughtful and serious attention.

I often reflect on my own reaction to this courteous, attractive young man. I had been brought up in an academic family in Cambridge whose members thought of themselves as liberals and good Democrats. But there was an inborn sense of anti-Catholicism and with it anti-Irish sentiment on the part of many middle-class, Protestant Cantabridgians, especially high-minded liberal types who felt that Irish politicians were ruining the city, appointing their relatives to jobs from city clerks to librarians, whether qualified or not. In a funny way, as a child, I always had the latent sense of being anti-Catholic and anti-Irish, in spite of the fact that I went to public school where most of my classmates and many of my friends were Irish Catholics. I guess I partook of the atmosphere of the times. It was an unthinking and deplorable prejudice. So when this attractive, well-bred, sophisticated young man came in, I was completely unprepared. I think it was at that moment that whatever prejudice was left in me melted away.

I was charmed by his courtesy, but I also remember thinking, in spite of his worldliness and sophistication, that there was something rather parochial about him. I had a feeling that he was in an alien atmosphere and wasn't comfortable. He had for me the somewhat dubious air of a young man who had wandered into a nest of pure-minded intellectuals, who, as far as he was concerned, spouted nonsense and foolish chitchat. And perhaps he was right, for, of course, he went on to defeat Henry Cabot Lodge the following November. The next time I met him the intellectuals were falling all over him.

As time went on, I had a sense that the Kennedys were not in the old-fashioned American political tradition. They were the wave of the future, something new and exotic on the political scene. I thought, if Truman had come to lunch that day, I would have had a greater feeling of affinity and familiarity with him than I had with Kennedy. Though they were both "ward" politicians in a sense (pay off your pals, etc.), I felt in a funny way that Kennedy belonged to a different political culture. But it was ridiculous that I was surprised, having lived in Massachusetts all my life. After all, it was just Kennedy-Massachusetts politics-as-usual gone national!

The Kennedy campaign of 1960 went on mostly outside my purview, though one episode sticks in my mind. I came home one day after an exhausting shopping trip to Filene's basement to find a donkey, deposited by Railway Express, on the front lawn, the "gift" of smart-aleck William F. Buckley Jr. to Arthur, in his role as a Democratic spokesman, I presumed. An impertinent note of unprintable sentiments accompanied the little creature. Needless to say, Arthur was off campaigning. The children were enchanted and the neighborhood young thronged about, taking turns sitting on the donkey's back as it stood stoically immovable. I was less enchanted. I had no forage except some dried-up lawn grass, and feed stores in Cambridge were non-existent. What to do? I tried to launch the recalcitrant beast into the back of the station wagon in order to deposit it with a good friend who lived in the country. But no matter how many hands pushed, the donkey would not budge.

Night was closing in when I had a sudden inspiration. My son Stephen, still underage, had signed for the donkey's delivery. I ran to the telephone and in tones of trumped-up outrage harangued the poor clerk at the Express office on this point, threatening suit if they did not come immediately and collect the illegal object. I had no idea if I had any legal grounds for all the palaver, but I must have sounded convincing. In the gathering dusk, the Railway Express pulled up and carried off the crated animal to the outfoxed arms of Mr. Buckley (I hoped). I later heard that the little beast had been christened Arthur.

There was a slight political crisis in the family a few weeks before the 1960 Democratic Convention. The primaries had hotted up, with Kennedy pulling off a successful coup in West Virginia against Hubert Humphrey. In the meantime, Stevenson was still shilly-shallying about a possible candidacy, encouraged by his female admirers like Mrs. Roosevelt. But even then one knew that his candidacy was unreal; no matter how devoted one was to the man, his time had passed. Arthur decided to come out for Kennedy while I stayed with Stevenson. Arthur claimed to be "nostalgically for Stevenson, ideologically for Humphrey, and realistically for Kennedy." But the announcement of Arthur's "defection" (and my support for Stevenson) appeared in the newspapers a few days after Adlai had dined with us at Irving Street, and Arthur had not yet told him. Although my husband had every right to change horses, as Adlai had denied any interest in running for a third time, I was furious that he had not informed Adlai, his dear friend, face to face.

I received a letter from Adlai a few days after the eruption in the newspapers and a subsequent backlash against Arthur by Stevenson loyalists who accused him of being an opportunist. "I am distressed by all that has happened," Adlai wrote, "and that I should be the cause of any embarrassment to Arthur whom I love as dearly as ever, as I am sure you both know. I think we will all survive the present distemper." At the same time, Arthur received a letter from Bobby Kennedy with a scrawled postscript, "Can't you control your own wife, or are you like me?"

After JFK received the nomination in Los Angeles, I, of course, enthusiastically supported him. I remember, that fall, before the election, going with Arthur to visit JFK and Jackie in Hyannis Port. After a spate of political palaver, we went for a short cruise on their powerboat. It was a beautiful, sunny day, and there was much chat and fun. I found Jackie delightful, but what impressed me most was that we had *oeuf en gelée* for lunch. Perhaps not the most significant memory to take away, though again it reveals my food-obsessed nature. But it did tell me something about Jackie's sophistication. Or my naïveté!

I recall the first time I became aware of Jackie's existence back in the 1950s. I saw a photograph of her in a newspaper dressed in a long, beautifully cut sheath of white satin, looking so chic. I remember thinking, "What style!" And this was in the days of gathered bouffant skirts and corsages, when we were all apt to look like a collection of Barbie dolls!

7

Washington Days

To HAVE LIVED FOR A MOMENT in the never-never land of high-level politics, so ephemeral and fleeting, was riveting, and I enjoyed every minute of it. How lucky I was to have been present in Washington during such an exciting time, during a fascinating administration, led by such a witty, charismatic, dashing, ironic, and utterly elusive President who surrounded himself with some extremely able people, some more able than they were wise.

What were the qualities in the young President that fascinated and mesmerized so many able men who flocked to serve in his administration? I think that some of these "brilliant" men often bestowed an exalted status on Kennedy, projecting their own ideal of what this "prince of a man" actually was, a true "intellectual" like themselves. One of them! An impossible dream come true, their country at last in the hands of a man of class, brains, style, educated in their milieu, and partaking of their values. And a Democrat in the bargain!

There was a roller-coaster atmosphere in those years. One felt that the administration reveled in crisis, and there were plenty of crises, some genuine and some invented for their own sake. I had a curious feeling that great decisions were made in an almost frivolous way, like the Bay of Pigs fiasco, which from my remote perch seemed to have been run by a bunch of hubris-mad teenagers, mostly Yale boys, who dominated the Central Intelligence Agency and who looked upon the Cuban enterprise and the catastrophe rather like a Harvard-Yale game they would win next time. After all, they had this huge United States Government as a plaything, so the analogy was not so far-fetched.

There was no question that the administration thrived on crisis and also on solutions to crisis. Solutions had to be on-the-double, overnight if possible, therefore confirming their heroic view of themselves. There seemed to have been too much reading of James Bond with few bars to the methods employed. In this atmosphere of derring-do, the CIA boys really felt their oats and were given their head. This was where the recklessness in the administration was most felt. But others courted danger, as we have subsequently learned, from the President on down. In fact, good horse sense seemed to be in short supply, and some of those counseling "slowing down and cooling it" were considered weak sisters and sidelined, an unpleasant treatment of self-respecting people, a kind of petty humiliation too often practiced by some of those in positions of power.

I had the curious sense that I was taking part in some sort of play, such was the feeling of unreality. And the beautiful city of Washington was the perfect backdrop. Something about the city reinforced the illusion, this one-company town with its official buildings with their heavy classical facades and impressive sites, like props in an ongoing drama. The cast of characters had their moments on stage, declaiming, posturing, plotting, dueling. And heading the cast were the charismatic hero and exotic heroine. Yet no one knew how the play would end!

I came down to join Arthur during the celebrations connected with the President's inauguration. We stayed with Joe Alsop, the Washington columnist and an old friend, in his Georgetown house for a night or two, which was an experience in itself. I remember sitting in his sunlit orangerie, a pretty little indoor garden room in his exquisite house (his taste was impeccable), and finding anchovy on the toast under my breakfast poached egg, and his telling us that he was going to marry Susan Mary Patten, the widow of his best friend Bill Patten, who had served in Paris for the State Department. I also remember years later sitting beside Truman Capote at a dinner party at Jackie Kennedy's New York apartment and his piping up in his ineffable voice, "Of course, Joe HAD to marry when the Kennedy Administration came in. You had to be married and have a hostess for all those parties—that was THE THING! And now the point for all THAT is gone! Too bad," he sighed

It was all pretty exotic, especially for one who had emerged from the daily grind of four children, one dog, innumerable guests, three meals a day, mountains of dishes and laundry, and one cleaning woman twice a week. In other words, real life!

The snow was coming down in buckets, traffic jams choked the streets, stalled cars and unavailable taxis made getting around almost impossible, but still the high spirits and excitement of the

Marian Cannon Schlesinger, Washington D.C., 1960s

revelers shushing through the snow drifts could not be downed. Inauguration Day turned out to be bitterly cold but brilliant. Robert Frost, the honored poet of the occasion, began to read one of his poems, but blinded by the sunlight, he decided to recite from memory "The Gift Outright." I could not help being reminded of conversations, martinis in hand, we used to have at the DeVotos' of a Sunday afternoon in Cambridge. On one occasion, Benny described what an egomaniacal monster Frost was in his human relations, not the paragon of virtue that I had surmised. I must say I was shocked. That he, a poet of such depths, should have flaws was almost unthinkable!

The President's speech was exhilarating, putting forth the much quoted words, "And so, my fellow Americans, ask not what your country can do for you; ask what you can do for your country." The whole occasion was thrilling, even though we shivered in our seats.

Because of the snow and general chaos, we missed out on one of the Presidential Balls where the President and Jackie, elegant in a sumptuous white satin gown, were greeted by ecstatic crowds. Instead, we went to a swinging cocktail party at the Phillip Grahams where for the first time one met NAMES: journalists, Senators, Washington lawyers (a type all their own), hostesses, newspaper editors, diplomats, and old friends from the years we spent in Washington before and after the war.

One evening we went to a party given by Jean and Stephen Smith, the President's sister and her husband, in a house almost next door to the one we finally rented on "O" Street in Georgetown. It was a party awash with the "beautiful people," with Kennedys as far as the eye could see. As usual, I was dropped off at the front door to sink or swim but soon fell into conversation with a most pleasant couple named McNamara, who seemed rather lost in the general confusion and feverish atmosphere. And so the nonstop social life in Washington began in January 1961, and my role as the perpetual onlooker was established.

With Arthur already hard at work in the White House, the children and I drove down to Washington in February 1961. It was a ghastly drive. A slippery sleet storm descended as we set forth. The overloaded station wagon broke down en route, and the dog was inadvertently left behind in some nameless motel at which we had put up out of desperation. She was finally retrieved, after floods of tears and howls of despair by the children.

We rented a crumbling old Federal Period house on "O" Street in Georgetown, full of faded charm, with a double living room and two fireplaces with beautifully carved mantles, the only signs of former elegance. I brought down some of my paintings from Cambridge and a few pieces of furniture, but mostly we lived with the tattered castoffs of our landlord. People came to see us not for our interior decor, I can promise you. On one side of the house was the Methodist parsonage with its amiable and respectable inmates, and on the other, the counselor of the Finnish Embassy and his wife, she by turns a would-be seductress or a snarling drunk. (She at one point tried to flirt over the back fence with Andy, age 13.) They spent a good deal of time drinking and fighting in violent Finnish (I presumed), thus adding to the general cacophony of the neighborhood.

We seemed not to have much luck with some of the diplomatic

set. In time it appeared that the Portuguese consul in Boston to whom we had rented our Cambridge house had turned the children's playroom on the third floor into a sort of seraglio, seducing Radcliffe girls left and right. The consul finally departed after Arthur had been in touch with the Portuguese Ambassador in Washington, but not before running off with some precious volumes from Arthur's library and deserting his wife and three children to fend for themselves in a strange land. It was reported that he ran off with one of the Radcliffe girls. To be sure, the consul was succeeded by a so-called respectable tenant, who turned out to be a sort of embodiment of the sixties, transforming the house into something of a hippie commune. For years after I returned to Cambridge, I came across people who had "enjoyed" her hospitality, or, rather, most of the time my hospitality, as she was so hippie she never paid her rent on time and sometimes not at all.

I was amused recently to be transported back to the sixties when a very scruffy, not very young man with a ponytail half way down his back rang the doorbell and asked politely if he could "see his old room." I was about to turn him away as he did not look too appetizing when he announced he had been one of Miss Brehm's protégées (as he put it so grandly) and wanted to see where he had spent so many happy hours. So many happy hours, no doubt, creating the unbelievable mess the house was in when I finally returned. So I let him in, and he apparently basked in the memory. At least he didn't steal the silver.

Georgetown still retained something of the feel of a small village in those days, before its present glitzy transformation. "M"

Street presented the somewhat shabby appearance of its origins as a nineteenth-century byway with dusty old hardware stores and plumbers shops, a five-and-ten-cent store, a frame shop, and an antique shop with a dark and strangely inviting interior full of wonderful pieces. Toward the Key Bridge, an even less respectable area, were a bar or two and some empty buildings falling into disrepair, though one, a faceless loft building, was said to host the secret goings-on of a CIA safe house. I remember going to some gloomy dive on "M" Street soon after we arrived in Washington and hearing the incomparable Miriam Makeba sing her South African click songs, and this was only a few blocks from where we lived.

Along Wisconsin Avenue, as it advanced up the hill toward Massachusetts Avenue, were arrayed long established little shops catering to the neighborhood: Martin's Tavern on the corner of "N" Street, Georgetown Pharmacy, a gathering spot where all sorts of juicy gossip was exchanged, Neam's Market, the Little Caledonia, selling chintzes and Italian pottery, Dorcas Hardin with her selection of smart clothes, and Per of Georgetown, a specialist in bouffant hairdos à la Jackie, where the chic ladies were coiffed for White House parties or diplomatic receptions. For a few years there was a movie theatre showing foreign films, specializing in Ingmar Bergman and other esoterica. Best of all was the wonderful Savile Book Shop on "P" Street, composed of two or three old buildings thrown together, so that one went up two or three steps to wander through the maze of overflowing shelves, a treasure-house of everything one might want to read. Alas, the Savile Book Shop has long since disappeared.

As spring came, Washington was revealed in all its beauty, with all its sights and sounds. It was hot to be sure, but lovely in the long warm afternoons and evenings, with the Japanese cherry trees along the tidal basin, the glorious swatches of color of the azaleas—oranges, pinks and fuchsias—the intoxicating smell of the box in the midday sun, the delicious odor of the honeysuckle perfuming the air, and the shirr of the locusts making their seventeen-year reappearance, their numbers enormous. With their revolting little black bodies strewn everywhere, it was difficult not to crush them underfoot with a sickening crunch.

The camellia bushes in the garden were in full bloom, one blood red, the other the purest white. Such exotica were never seen in the backyards of Cambridge. A pair of cardinals nested in the magnolia tree next to the garden wall, and the scarlet flash of the male flitting through the glossy leaves was gorgeous. But it was their distinct "O" call that will always remind me of Washington. So poignant! Of course there were other sounds, less poignant, like the sirens of the police cars chasing delinquents down "M" Street late at night, or the roar of airplanes on the flight path down the Potomac to the National Airport, which made conversation in the garden in the evening something of a shouting match.

On a perfect sunny spring afternoon I went to the Phillips Collection for the first time in many years. I was reminded of the time when we lived in Washington during the war and a friend and I used to steal away, leaving our children with good-natured "colored" ladies while borrowing their D.C. bus passes to make the break for it. Sometimes we went downtown and moseyed through the aisles of Woodward & Lothrop or Garfinckel's, or had our hair done, but more often we made a beeline for the Phillips Collection. I had never seen a Klee or a Vuillard or a Bonnard before and had hardly heard of Matisse and Picasso and never of Juan Gris or Braque. They were still there, reminding me how exhilarating and puzzling my first sight of them had been, when I thought the large Bonnards, the gorgeously colored *The Open Window* and *The Riviera*, were simply a mess (how one's taste changes), but immediately responded to the Klees and to the Vuillard painting of *The Woman Sweeping*. For years I could remember the pattern of the old woman's wrapper against the busy brown wallpaper of the typical dreary French interior.

The great Victorian mansion near Dupont Circle was much the same in the 1960s, although a modern addition had been added to house the Rothkos and Klines. The Rouaults still hung in the dark oak-paneled library to the right of the hall, like stained-glass windows in a dim cathedral. The Phillipses had unerring eyes. They collected nothing but the best: the perfect little Degas of *Women Combing Their Hair*, the Corot Italian landscape, the magnificent Renoir, *Luncheon of the Boating Party*, the mysterious Rouaults, the interesting De Staels and Mondrians, the great Manet, *Ballet Español*, the Van Gogh, *Public Garden at Arles*, and so many others.

The Phillips Collection was THE aesthetic resource and still is as far as I am concerned. In contrast to the miles of marble floors and the host of people at the National Gallery, there is something about the intimacy of the setting and the domestication of the art, not to mention the carpeting at the Phillips, which seems to concentrate one's attention in a significant way. I always thought those rooms provided a perfect setting for a tryst, a romantic spot in this strangely sexless city (despite all the goings-on), where an elegantly tailored gentleman could meet his beautiful mistress, exquisitely gowned in pale chiffon, a throw of sable over her shoulder, a wide-brimmed hat on her ash blonde hair. Every cliché imaginable. Very Henry James-y. But how unlike the Kennedy scene. Discretion seemed to be out the window. Who cared? No one had mistresses any more, a recherché concept. Babes were more the style!

But the serious business of Washington was, of course, politics. The determining factor was power, and the exercise of it seemed to take place strictly offstage. All the huge decisions taken by Congress and the President, one felt, were taken in a kind of enclosed inner sanctum while the American public waited to discover its fate.

Speaking of such, I seem of late to have become interviewee of the month for several people writing books about the Kennedy Administration. I should have thought that by this time everything on the subject had already been said. They were certainly scraping the bottom of the barrel if they felt the urge to come and talk to me, a very peripheral and bemused onlooker. I had done an oral history for the Kennedy Library, which wasn't as worshipful as some, and perhaps that was where they got the idea that I had something to say. But even so, since I lived through the period, they thought I had some feeling for its "essence." I think they had some romantic idea that great decisions were taken by great men about matters of peace and war in distinguished salons presided over by fashionable and beautiful women, à la Henry Adams's *Democracy*. Of course, the whole idea is ridiculous. Decisions like the Bay of Pigs or the Cuban Missile Crisis were made, one can be sure, without the intervention of gorgeous saloniers. I was amused by some of these interviewers. They asked questions and if you waited long enough they answered their own questions. And if you waited even longer, you started asking them questions, and the whole history of their lives came tumbling out.

Speaking of "saloniers," the Kennedy Administration had an unusually sparkling bevy of smart women and fashionable hostesses such as Kay Graham, Evangeline Bruce, the wife of David Bruce, our Ambassador to Great Britain, and Susan Mary Alsop. I always felt that Evangeline would have been the perfect model for the heroine of Henry Adams's novel. A great beauty in the Edwardian mode with her swan neck and elegant bearing, she was reserved, somewhat narcissistic, intellectual in a bookish way and at the same time somehow impenetrable, with her coterie of friends, political, artistic and otherwise, with whom she surrounded herself.

I knew her in Cambridge before the war when she took special courses at Harvard's Fogg Museum, "special courses" especially designed for *jeunes filles bien élevées*, those debutantes who in today's world would be off to Harvard or Brown or whichever is the smart university to attend at the moment. When the war began, she came to Washington and worked as a secretary to Francis Biddle, the Attorney General. I wouldn't have thought she was much of a secretary, rather an exotic element around the office,

Ed Prichard, one of the brilliant Harvard Law School graduates dispatched by Felix Frankfurter to work in the New Deal, then an assistant to Biddle, is said to have fallen madly in love with her. What a wonderful picture, this huge, fat Kentuckian, a witty colossus, in love with this exquisitely beautiful girl. However, this exquisitely beautiful girl was making her way in the world. And what a way she made. In the course of the war, she went to London where she met and married David Bruce, high in the FDR circles. Bruce had first been married to a Mellon, the daughter of Andrew Mellon, founder of the National Gallery. When David became Ambassador to Great Britain, Evangeline became the paradigm of an Ambassadress with her elegant taste in dress and decor like so many swan-necked beauties painted by Reynolds and Gainsborough, surrounded by King Charles spaniels. Once when I stayed with her at the Embassy in London, I remember a luncheon when all her dogs were present either at her side or under the table and happily fed by their mistress. I felt that in some ways they were her closest companions.

The parties at Phillip and Kay Graham's had a quality all their own. There were Phil's pals from the early days, the bright young lawyers who streamed to Washington as law clerks to Supreme Court justices, especially the protegés of Felix Frankfurter, men like the civil-rights lawyer Joe Rauh and Jim Rowe, a special assistant in the Roosevelt Administration and an intimate of Vice President Johnson. There were members of the Kennedy Administration like Mac Bundy and George Ball, pundits like Walter Lippmann and Marquis Child, has-been politicians, ex-CIA honchos like Allen Dulles, journalists, especially those representing the *London Times* and *The Economist*, International Monetary Fund officials like the father of the actress Helena Bonham Carter (I did a portrait of her three-year-old brother in Washington; I wonder what became of it?), intellectuals, artists, musicians, old friends to whom they were invariably loyal. The list goes on and on, the eclecticism a wonder.

Another mix of the fashionable and the political took place at Joe and Susan Mary Alsop's beautiful Georgetown house with its elegant Chinese screens and Sung scrolls. Joe was the irascible, opinionated columnist for the *Washington Post* whose columns were read every day to find out the inside dope. You were certain to meet the latest luminaries at his dinner parties, occasions rather overly dominated by Joe himself with his insistent barking voice and absolute opinions leaving little room for conversation except on his terms. But it was always so diverting, the ladies so beautifully dressed, the interior decor so chic, the food delicious, and the atmosphere so highly charged that one might be a witness to a "confrontation" of a political or ideological sort, as with a roar Joe challenged some hapless guest, a challenge that in the old days might have ended in a duel.

To be sure, those were the days when the archaic custom of the separation of the ladies after dinner was de rigueur in some settings. I thought it quite silly but did not mind as some of the ladies were very interesting or their chatter diverting and most of the male talk had already been reported in the morning edition of the *Washington Post*.

At home I was often drafted to give stag luncheons in the garden for Arthur's colleagues and visiting firemen, including, for example, on one occasion, Walter Lippmann, Ted Sorensen, James Wechsler of the *New York Post*, Richard Rovere of the *New Yorker*, and Juan Bosch, at that time president-elect of the Dominican Republic. Since I was the only female partaking of the conversation, I happily thwarted the "separation."

Of course, there were other hostesses like Lorraine Cooper, the wife of Senator John Sherman Cooper of Kentucky, who had carried off her somewhat backwoodsy husband in a typical Washington way and put him in the social whirl. The wife of the Indian Ambassador, Fori Nehru, was another potent character and, considering the fact that she was Hungarian by birth, more Indian than the Indians. There was always in the wings the feisty old lady, Alice Roosevelt Longworth, who I felt had made the same "witty" remarks and cracked the same jokes over so many years with always a new and appreciative audience. And, to be sure, there was Lady Bird Johnson, ever the poised and gracious hostess.

It was good that the prosaic life of home and children somewhat tied me to the ground. Otherwise I might have been off into the firmament with never a backward glance. I must say I felt guilty at times to be in a privileged position in relation to the administration when at the same time I was casting rather a critical eye at some of the goings-on, the hype, the recklessness, and the license. Though I took a dim view of some of these shenanigans, there were of course many able, serious people in the administration. Interestingly, many of them had originally worked for Adlai Stevenson when governor of Illinois or when he ran for president: George Ball, Newt Minow, Ken Galbraith, Bill

Wirtz, Bill Blair, and many others. Stevenson attracted nothing but the best, as far as I could see. I liked the way he treated those who worked for him, respectful of them as individuals, never patronizing, whereas the Kennedys had a tendency to turn people into courtiers. The Kennedys were pretty tough customers. If you were not with them lock, stock, and barrel, you were out in the cold. Perhaps that is the loyalty demanded by all politicians when they finally gain power, but it was certainly true in their case.

One evening I sat at the left of the President at a small dinner party in the pretty upstairs dining room of the White House.

The Schlesinger family: Marian, Andrew, Kathy, Chrissie and Stephen, c. 1960

We talked about Massachusetts politics. I thought it rather sly of him to suggest that Arthur's grasp of politics was on such an exalted level that he did not realize what ward and precinct politics were all about. The President obviously recognized in me the ward-and-precinct type who rang the doorbells and theoretically got out the vote.

Golf seemed to have been the relaxation of the Eisenhower years, but in the Kennedy years tennis was the sport of choice. We all played, from Bob McNamara and Ethel Kennedy on down. We ladies were especially busy. We played on the White House court, which in those days was in rather ratty condition. One of the policy decisions that does not appear in most of the history books was whether the Interior Department or the National Lawn Tennis Association could be conned into filling the cracks and generally resurfacing the court. Which did it, I don't know, but eventually it was done. We played on the courts of the St. Albans School with a view of the National Cathedral up the hill. We played on Ethel's court at Hickory Hill. She was a fierce competitor. As I wrote in a column about Washington women tennis players for the *Washington Post*, "The only way to beat her is in the last few hours before her labor begins and even that isn't a sure thing."

Private courts were a special part of tennis life in Washington. One of the great institutions was the permanent tennis party that went on from early April to the end of October at the court of Jean and Al Friendly in Georgetown. Al was the managing editor of the *Washington Post*. Those who weren't playing tennis would sit under the trees sipping iced tea and playing bridge.

What a delicious way to spend a hot summer afternoon!

I joined the Woman's National Democratic Club and had the fun of introducing Art Buchwald for his first Washington speech since his arrival from Paris where he had written his popular column for *The Paris Herald Tribune*. "The wonderful thing about Art Buchwald," I remarked, "is that he is the greatest ANTI-HOKUM artist since H.L. Mencken and Groucho Marx. He carries on in his columns the best natured, sharpest, and deadliest assault on the cant, the pretensions, and the absurdities of our national life being written anywhere today. Nothing is sacred, from the President on down, not excluding the Joint Chiefs of Staff, TV, civil rights, Vietnam, the CIA, the New Left, the New Right, Motherhood, the Kennedys, even that sacrosanct body, the Teenagers of America, all subjects for his high-spirited mayhem." The audience even laughed at my jokes.

I fixed up a studio in the back of the house and painted a number of children's portraits (perhaps 25 in all), among them, the three charming daughters of the Newton Minows—the head of the FCC—the yellow-slickered grandson of another friend, and a double portrait of the Walter Lippmanns's granddaughters. I even sent a little watercolor of a red horse to Jackie as a thank-you note for some occasion and got a cute note back, all exaggerations to be sure, but welcome even so. "Neither of us can get over the fantastic horse. I have never heard Jack rave so about a picture, so the sobbing sail boat I gave him for his birthday was treated with the same admiration as John's birthday card!"

I wonder what happened to that picture? It certainly was not included in the famous Sotheby's sale of Jackie's estate, not

*Marian in her studio working on a portait of Martha, Mary
and Nell Minow with Chrissie looking on, 1962*

exactly in the same class as Ari's jeweled baubles. No doubt
long since thrown out with the trash. Much as what happened
to a small portrait I did of Averell Harriman, which I thought
quite good, which was inadvertently disposed of by a wayward
maid. However, I had a show of paintings and drawings at a
Georgetown gallery, and the powers that be came out in droves.
The gallery was run by a funny little monkey of a man who was
in a state of euphoria over the turnout.

Portrait of Wendy and Katrina vanden Heuvel by MCS, 1964

Culture seemed to be breaking out all over. We went with the President and Jackie to a concert by the National Symphony Orchestra and sat in the President's box. I have completely forgotten the program but remember that we left at the intermission, the point apparently having been made. Naturally, I wore the wrong dress, much too bare, while Jackie was her usual elegant self in an evening suit of rich brocade. I must have been

President and Mrs. Kennedy with their guests, Mr. and Mrs. Arthur Schlesinger, as they attended the second half of the National Symphony concert last night at Constitution Hall. This was the opening night of the 31st season for the National Symphony. The conductor is Dr. Howard Mitchell. —Star Staff Photo.

The Kennedys and Arthur and Marian Schlesinger at a concert by the National Symphony Orchestra, the Washington Star, 1961

regarded as some sort of cultural maven of the administration, as I was bid to all sorts of events, among them a concert by French musicians playing Bach fugues on rows of glasses filled with various levels of water, the sound evoked by the rubbing of moist fingers around the lips of the glasses producing a delicate moan. There was some wonderful music in Washington in those days, especially the intimate concerts at Dumbarton Oaks, the great mansion with its beautiful gardens dominating the heights of Georgetown. Almost as interesting as the music was the audience, a cross-section of Washington society from diplomats and journalists to writers and artists, a legislator or two, Washington hostesses, Supreme Court justices, and the rest of us who were fortunate to be invited. Not many members of the administration attended as far as I could see. Culture was a sometime thing, I presumed, and there were more important things to do than go to concerts at Dumbarton Oaks.

But the big aesthetic experience was the importation and showing of the *Mona Lisa* at the National Gallery in early 1963, a prime excuse for the ladies to put on their most lavish gowns and sally forth. The reception launching the exhibit was rather a lark though slightly absurd—no one could hear what was said and people were jostling each other like fans at a football game to "get closer to the picture." No matter, the city was well on its way to developing into a cultural capital from a sort of parochial small town, although it had had for so many years the foundations on which to build: the National Gallery, the Freer Gallery, the Phillips Collection, the Smithsonian, the Library of Congress, the National Symphony, and many other well established institutions. Yet the atmosphere created by the Kennedy Administration set Washington on its way!

8

The Kennedy Experience

THE WHITE HOUSE WAS the site of many distinguished gatherings, from dinners for Nobel Prize winners to a concert by Pablo Casals. Gorgeously redecorated under Jackie's connoisseur's eye, the Blue and the Green rooms were also the scene of wonderful White House dances. My first White House experience was at one of these dances. I seem to have always been left at the front door to fend for myself but actually didn't mind that much, as I more and more saw myself as the bemused onlooker, delighting in the antics of the young and the beautiful. A bevy of fashionable lovelies were imported from New York, rather placing us stodgy Washington types in the shade. We had drinks beforehand with the President and Jackie in the family quarters. It was like being at the chicest cocktail party, all the ladies exquisitely dressed (or, I should say, "overdressed") and coiffed to a fare-thee-well, beehives as far as the eye could see. My own dress, made up of some glorious heavy pink satin brocade bought many years ago in Peking, had been "run up" by a friend's "little Italian dressmaker." To be "lent" someone's dressmaker was the height of favor, I discovered, being unaware as I was of such fine points of status!

Jackie looked *très soignée* and attractive and with her breathy voice made us all welcome. I sensed in her a sardonic tongue and a sharp eye that didn't miss much. After we had all assembled, when the President came in, the effect was spectacular. Such an attractive man, and besides, the charisma attached to the office was enough to make one swoon. And I am not the swooning type.

By the end of the evening, suffering from a combination of powerful martinis and sheer excitement, I could not account for whole chunks of time. But I recall an amusing exchange with the artist Mary Meyer and her sister Tony Bradlee, wife of Ben Bradlee (later editor of the *Washington Post*), as we retired to the lady's powder room and mutually complained about being wall flowers in the face of the youthful beauties from New York. Years later, when it was revealed that Mary Meyer was at the time having a passionate affair with the President, I was amused to remember that I had been genially bamboozled by that attractive woman. Alas, she was cruelly murdered in 1964 as she jogged along the C&O canal, a murder with mysterious overtones and never solved. I reflected that, in regard to Mary Meyer, the President had shown such excellent taste, for she was a person of talent, beauty, and class.

Not all parties were as decorous as those at the White House. The parties at Hickory Hill, home of Robert and Ethel Kennedy, were something else again. Not only awash with children, dogs, and a generous cross section of members of the administration from Robert McNamara to the astronaut John Glenn, from cabinet members to the roster of smart lawyers from the Justice Department that Kennedy gathered around him, but also awash with guests happily pushed into the swimming pool fully dressed. The resulting splash became something of a touchstone, defining the go-go atmosphere of the times.

I think Ethel and Bobby in their hospitable way created a sense of family for many members of the administration. As an extended family there were often going-away parties for those leaving the administration to return to "civilian" life. I remember one given for Mike Forrestal, son of Truman's Secretary of Defense, James Forrestal, who had worked as an assistant to McGeorge Bundy on the National Security Council. I wrote the following poem as a going away present:

> Oh, Mike, don't go
> You'll leave us flat
>
> No one to call us
> On the mat.
>
> Who'll cite the book
> On Tran Van Huc?
>
> Who'll ring the gong
> On the Viet Cong?
>
> Who'll tell LeMay
> He's got feet of clay?
>
> Who'll bring Walt
> To a verbal halt?

Who'll come clean
With George and Dean?

Who'll scatter flack
On Bill and Mack?

Who'll make it plain
To Lynda Bayne

That God and Daddy
Aren't the same?

And, Ladies, who will eat
At that empty seat?

Don't go dear Mike
To the private sector

We need you here
As our protector.

Who cares about money?
Who cares about pearls?

Who cares about parties
With beautiful girls?

Who cares about clients
With plenty of dough?

Think twice, Mike
Before you go.

Cause there's always a chance
That if you stay

You could lower the boom
On L.B.J.

When the go-go atmosphere got a bit thick, the saving grace for me was the enchanting Katherine Biddle. Her husband, Francis Biddle, had been Attorney General during the Roosevelt Administration and was as delightful in his way as she was in hers. An intellectual, a poet, a beautiful woman full of ironic wit (the Kennedy Administration was not long on irony except for the President; perhaps politics is inimical to it), Katherine was a fount of humor and good sense in the middle of the maelstrom, after all the kidding and horsing around that was typical of the Kennedy scene.

It was a joy and a relaxation to go to their house in Georgetown for tea in the cool, dark living room, full of rather hideous paintings by George Biddle, Francis's artist brother (a very nice man but not to my taste in art), as well as family portraits, overflowing book cases, and tea and cocktails served by an ancient maid who had been attending the Biddles for decades. The dinners were delightful, too: the same ancient servitors passing the soup in silver serving dishes, slightly tarnished, worn but elegant monogrammed linen napkins, and, sitting around the table, rather worn and elegant antique figures, literary and political, from another era. Such was the fate, I feared, of the survivors of each political generation as they slowly faded into oblivion. The generations piled up like so many geologic ages, and by sedulous use of pick and shovel, historians, I was sure, could find relics as far back as the Harding Administration and even earlier.

I thought the Hickory Hill seminars, so-called after the home of Robert Kennedy and, in fact, a project of his, were rather an intellectual quick fix. Everyone was there who "mattered" and all very serious-minded and attentive. The "big guns" were produced and it was hoped that the audience would have "great thoughts." No doubt a harmless exercise, but so Kennedyish, the whole of Western Thought in eight hour-long seminars. Such speakers as Freddie Ayer, the English philosopher, who at the least was extremely difficult, was one of the "stars." I do not remember what he was talking about, but something he said got under Ethel's skin, and she blurted out, "Oh, well, I believe in God!" or words to that effect. I remember Bobby turning to her and virtually telling her to "shut up." I do not remember whether he used those actual words, but the implication was, "Keep your mouth shut. What do you know about anything?" And this was supposed to be a "learning experience"!

Of course, they never had anyone speak who wasn't out of the top drawer, as it were. Nothing but the best, no matter how in-comprehensible. The whole enterprise seemed to me rather self-conscious though benign, something like Voltaire at the Court of Frederick the Great. And it was rather like a court, with intel-lectuals, philosophers, and courtiers in attendance.

The kidding that went on, especially in the case of Bobby and Ethel, was extremely tiresome. But in time I began to think that it was their way of communicating with each other and with other people. It was something the President did too. I remem-ber going to the White House for cocktails on some occasion and Jackie coming into the room wearing a very good look-ing suit that was obviously *très cher* (Chanel, I think) and his drawing attention to it and saying, "Well, how much did you pay for that, Jackie?", half kidding and half in mock irritation. I finally concluded that the kidding was not only a form of communication, but also a way of keeping people off balance and at arm's length. In other words, keeping things under control. As for conversation, it did not exist. Perhaps that was asking too much!

In the winter of 1962, I went along with Arthur and George McGovern on the second leg of their Food for Peace mission, joining them in Tokyo. They had been in Argentina and were en route to Hong Kong and India. We spent a day or two in Hong Kong and I recalled the last time I had been there thirty years before when it was an outpost of the British Empire. It was now almost unrecognizable, already beginning its fantastic growth, burgeoning with population and building. And I remember thinking to myself, "Once the Chinese get going, watch out! They are so smart and so pragmatic!"

I fell completely under the spell of India, a weird and wonderful country, foretold for me many years earlier by the illustrations of Arthur Rackham and Edmund Dulac in the fairy tale volumes that we as children devoured. For an artist it was a land of intoxication, the ravishing colors of the women's saris, the marvelous architecture, Muslim tombs, Rajput palaces and crumbling Hindu temples, the variety of religions, Sikhs, Hindus, Jains, Muslims, sadus with their bodies smeared with ashes, Buddhist monks in brilliant orange robes, and the dun reaches of the Rajastani desert. It was a country overwhelming not only in its beauty but in its excruciating poverty, its burgeoning population, and its intractable problems. For those who could not bear the sight of so much human suffering, I said, stay away!

Udaipur, India *by MCS, 1962*

As I wrote to my sister, "In New Delhi we stayed with the Galbraiths at the United States Embassy where as Ambassador he's probably the tallest man in India. Some Sikh would probably challenge that!" At one point I accompanied Kitty Galbraith and Florence Mahoney (an assistant to the philanthropist and art collector Mary Lasker, who was traveling with the Food for Peace mission group) to Jaipur and Udaipur to make arrangements for the upcoming trip to India of Jackie and her sister Lee Radziwell. There we were entertained at lunch by the Maharajah of Udaipur, a wizened, elderly man, who was rather a disappointment when I thought of my romantic idea of what a Maharajah ought to look like. However, his palace could not have been more

Marian on the terrace of the Maharajah's palace, Udaipur, 1962

wonderful. White, white, white, with domes and balustrades, peacocks sunning themselves on its terraces, and a lake lapping at its foundations. In the middle of the lake "floated" the Lake Palace, a delicious wreck of a confection, all frilly white marble and embellished with more onion-hatted domes and balustrades. I remember Florence Mahoney with her sharp and entrepreneurial eye suggesting to the Maharajah that "something should be done to develop that wonderful Lake Palace." She was ahead of her time. It was some years before the world would discover the wonders of India, turning it into the present tourist mecca and the Lake Palace into a beautiful *de luxe* hotel.

I coveted the portraits of the Maharajah's ancestors, which lined the walls of the dining room where we had lunch. They were my type of portraiture, flat but with each face individually differentiated, and the fabulous clothes and jeweled turbans meticulously painted. And I wondered at the paper-thin sheets of silver that adorned our custard like dessert. To eat or not to eat? I ate and afterwards I learned that sheets of silver on one's dessert were the height of elegance. And so one learned something new every day.

Florence Mahoney was a great character, a New York PR type who once worked for Elizabeth Arden. She was full of beans and initiative and a demon shopper with a good eye for fabrics, jewelry, antiques, and *objets* of all sorts. She knew her way around! I simply gave myself over to her and she led me by the nose from one extravagance to the next. In Jaipur, with her usual lively initiative she arranged a visit to the shop of the chief jeweler of the Maharajah where naturally we were led immediately into the back room, the Sanctum Sanctorum (no idling along the way). There, rubies, emeralds, sapphires and diamonds were poured out onto velvet cushions for our delectation. You felt like thrusting your hands into the heaps of jewels and letting them drop through your fingers. It was like a scene from *The Arabian Nights*. Florence Mahoney bought liberally, and even I bought five small cabochon emeralds, which I had set in a ring when I got back to Delhi. But with my usual bad luck before I got home two of the emeralds had fallen out and were lost. Later I got a good jeweler in Provincetown to augment the three remaining emeralds and design a charming ring, which I wear to this day.

In Calcutta we joined up with Bobby and Ethel Kennedy and their retinue of reporters and aides, as they were making their way around the world en route to Italy and Germany. Bobby had been heckled viciously in Japan by radical students at Waseda University, but by tactfully and firmly stating his views he had succeeded in turning the tide and winning the day, according to Tokyo newspapers. We flew on to Rome where the Kennedy party at its adolescent worst created mayhem at Alfredo's restaurant when Ethel rode a motor scooter between the tables. Or so it was reported

I was present at one of the most embarrassing occasions I ever witnessed at the dinner given by the mayor of West Berlin, Willy Brandt, before Bobby's speech at the Free University of Berlin on February 22. The dinner was very Germanic, stiff, formal, and heavy like the surroundings. There were thirty or more guests, all important people in the government. Teddy Kennedy had joined the group, and in the middle of the dinner Bobby arose and announced, "Well, whose birthday do you think it is today?" Bobby continued in this awful kidding vein and then announced, "Teddy's going to sing some songs from South Boston." So Teddy, the birthday boy, and his sidekick got up in the middle of the banquet and sang "When Irish Eyes Are Smiling" and "Danny Boy," among others. Teddy was obviously high and the tension was almost unbearable. (Of course, Teddy finally grew up and became our excellent and irreplaceable Senator from Massachusetts.)

The Kennedys often did this sort of thing, turning so many occasions into little private parties of their own, full of private jokes and silly by-play. They were so self-centered that if something happened to them, then it had to be of overwhelming importance to everyone concerned whether it be the burghers of Berlin or the shopkeepers of Rome. It took me a long time to get over this example of bad manners. Except for the rather awful banquet, the rest of the evening went off without a hitch. Bobby spoke very well and the audience was enthusiastic. I guess my reaction did not sour my relations with Bobby for I went on to campaign for him at his request in his run for the presidency in 1968 in Indiana, Oregon, and California.

"Social notes from all over," I wrote to a friend early in 1963. "I've sat next to some pretty 'big names' at dinner lately and I can tell you there is many a one with feet of clay under the table. That has been one of the most interesting conclusions I have come to over the months, and I am amazed that we are as well governed as we are, considering some of the nerds that seem to be in charge. Of course there are some pretty smart cookies, but still there is a parochialism that I found surprising, especially among the men."

Having divested myself of such disagreeable observations, I went on to remark that "journalists and newspaper men are the most fun, humorous and sharp. And of course there are exceptions as always in the Executive branch and in Congress. Speaking of social notes from all over, yesterday was the annual cocktail party of the Walter Lippmann's where the bores are not necessarily invited unless they are the LATEST THING. There's always much to-do over the two standard poodles, which sashay around the living room, much cooed over by Helen Lippmann. She rather treated Lippmann himself like some precious piece of porcelain, wrapped in her protective covering, his time allotted, and she the perfect keeper of the shrine. But the company was great. You get the picture.

"But if you're not interested in politics, forget it! Fortunately, I'm fascinated by the whole scene; every nuance noted, discussed, ruminated upon, who's going to be appointed and why and under whose aegis. Finally the appointment goes through after ruthless examination in Congress, newspapers, TV, etc. Then no sooner appointed, the knives come out, wielded by the same people who called for the appointment in the first place, to tear him down. Interesting! Amazing anything gets done." How little seems to have changed through the subsequent decades.

Even the terrible assassination of President Kennedy did not stop the forward flow of politics. For only a moment the internecine battles for power ceased, and one was forced to reflect on what a pass our nation had come to. But then life took up its erstwhile pace and all the ongoing problems reasserted themselves. In the emotional aftermath of Kennedy's death, the usually intractable Congress passed the civil rights legislation begun under the Kennedy Administration and enacted under the overwhelming pressure of Johnson's legislative know-how.

In the face of Johnson's remarkable domestic political achievements, I reflect how bizarre it was that four years after he took office, his very name was anathema to so many over his expansion of the Vietnam War. The fact that I took part in a light-hearted campaign for his reelection in 1964 against the bomb-dropping figure of Barry Goldwater seems amazing to me. We were still living in Washington. Arthur had resigned from the Johnson Administration and was writing his book on

*Scottie Lanahan, Marian Schlesinger, and Ceci Carusi with
Lieutenant Governor Wilson W. Wyatt, Louisville, Kentucky, 1964*

the Kennedy years, *A Thousand Days*. The Women's Division of
the Democratic National Committee decided to dispatch four
women, Ceci Carusi, Mary Janney, "Scottie" Lanahan and me
to campaign for the national ticket in Michigan, Wisconsin
and Minnesota. We were billed as the "Four Women From
Washington," which I guess was supposed to sound formidable
out in the boondocks. We may have sounded formidable, but, as
a matter of fact, although we had all been active in Democratic
politics, none of us had ever campaigned on such a scale before.
However, a little thing like that couldn't stop us, as we set forth
in a state of exhilaration, having boned up on issues, domestic
and foreign, economic and military.

We set off in a Ford station wagon lent by the wife of a Ford
Motor Company executive (she a closet Democrat; he, I presume,

either an unsuspecting Republican or a besotted husband). Accompanied by local Democratic candidates, we spoke in high school gymnasiums, dark motel pubs redolent with the smell of stale beer and cigarette smoke, and private homes where we were given the royal treatment as we brought fire and brimstone upon the head of the hapless Goldwater and painted Johnson as a man of exemplary compassion and peace. We traveled the length of Michigan and across the Upper Peninsula to Marquette, spying the great red iron ore boats along the huge jetties reaching out into Lake Superior, then continued down through Wisconsin to Minnesota, ending up in Minneapolis.

Minnesota produced many non-political emotions. I was reminded that my great-grandmother came to St. Paul in the mid-nineteenth century from Maine, a widow with two children, who was appointed the first principal of the St. Paul High School in the 1860s. I am sure she would have approved of my political activities. For "Scottie" Lanahan, the daughter of Zelda and Scott Fitzgerald, it was the first time she had seen the place where her father had spent his childhood. A group of her father's friends, hospitable and graying, entertained us at White Bear Lake, the site of some of his most poignant stories. "Scottie" was our domestic specialist, eloquent to be sure, but like the rest of us, slightly skewing some of her statistics. But we were fast movers, getting out of town before we could be too closely questioned.

I do not want to leave the impression that we were a bunch of bubble heads, for on the whole I think we held our own, stating the facts and making cogent arguments. "Scottie" was not only our domestic maven, but also our chief news gatherer, being a compulsive newspaper buyer and reader. No small town newspaper was too negligible for her appetite. Often, at the end of the day, when the rest of us threw ourselves, exhausted, down on our beds in our motel room, she would retire to the bathroom to finish reading every bit of news print acquired along the way. The fact of a newspaper unread before she went to sleep was unthinkable for her.

Another of our number suffered from a different neurosis. Mary Janney couldn't drive across bridges. The Middle West seemed to be criss-crossed by small and large streams and rivers. It fell to me to change places with her and drive whenever we came to one of these dread barriers. Once across, she would blithely take the wheel and barrel through the countryside at speeds up to 80 or 90 miles an hour, which had me cowering in my seat developing a neurosis of my own.

One episode I remember with some amusement took place in a small community near Green Bay, Wisconsin. The turnout was significantly larger than usual, much to our pleasure, but when we began to speak there was palpable dismay in the poker faces of the gathered farmers and their wives, and then the audience began to melt away. It seemed they had been promised Miss America, Bess Myerson, and the sight of Four Women From Washington, no matter how worthy, was not enough!

Whether we made any difference in the outcome of the election, I do not know and rather doubt, although we may have helped elect the first Democratic Representative ever from Northern Michigan. At least we raised curiosity in some heavily Republican districts, drank gallons of coffee, and sometimes made policy that President Johnson might well have listened to and benefited by.

My friend Jane McBain and I went on a trip to Spain in late 1964. Jane, the daughter of Hearst's lawyer, a well-heeled divorcee, had come from San Francisco to Washington to live it up with the rest of the Kennedy coterie. She was so Irish, gregarious (she knew EVERYBODY), generous, warm-hearted, and temperamental, but with a sharp eye that did not miss a trick—a certain type of predatory female that proliferated in Washington in those days and no doubt still does. I was so fond of her. She finally "carried off" Marquis Childs, the columnist and author of an influential book, *Sweden: The Middle Way*, at that time a widower, whom she married at the end of the Johnson years and returned with to San Francisco. I remember calling on them in their gorgeous apartment on Nob Hill and having the feeling that he was to be sure very satisfied with his life but at the same time bemused by it, as though he really did not know what had happened to him.

In Madrid, Jane and I stayed at the Embassy with the Angier Biddle Dukes, old friends of Jane and known to me because I had done a portrait of their son when they lived in Washington. I especially remember two things from that visit. One was the wonderful trip we took in the early spring to Segovia, Avila and Toledo: the marvelous barren countryside with just a suggestion of green in the fields, the streams without verges overflowing their banks, running on top of the land, the dark green ovoid-shaped oaks dotting the landscape, and the herds of sheep on the stark brown plains. It was very raw and cold in spite of the brilliant sunshine, and you could not help remembering the bitterness and hardship of the fighting which went on all over the country during the Spanish Civil War, perhaps some of it in these very fields.

I was reminded of what Spain had been like when we as a family visited it when I was 17 years old in 1930. My father had lectured in Barcelona and Madrid at the invitation of his fellow physiologist, the politician Juan Negrín, later prime minister under the Loyalists. I wish I had been more aware of what I was looking at then for we saw Spain as it must have been for centuries. I have a flashing memory of seeing a little village festival with the women in brilliant costumes, of going to a bullfight in Madrid which I hated, of the bold gypsies living in the caves of Andalusia, of having suckling pig to eat, and so much more, but have no memory of going to the Prado, though I suppose we did.

But this time, the Prado! What a marvelous experience it was for me, seeing for the first time so many Goyas that I had only seen in reproductions as well as the other riches of that greatest of all museums.

The second memory of that visit to Madrid was going to a fabulous party at the sumptuous apartment of one Carmen Marañón. She had been the daughter of my father's colleague Dr. Gregorio Marañón, a member of a very distinguished Spanish family and a fellow physiologist, whom we had visited in 1930. He was later one of the early movers in the Spanish revolution, but like so many beginners he retired from the movement when it was taken over and transformed by the Communists. I remember our going to their house and meeting the children of the family in their pretty quarters where they were taken care of by an English nanny. Carmen was my age and for some reason or other we became "instant friends," and I corresponded with her, one teenager to another as it were, for a few years after I got back to America. But that was a whole lifetime ago and I had completely lost track of her. I had heard vaguely that she had married a rich older man, obviously a Franco partisan.

Anyway, when I asked Robin Duke whether she had ever heard of Carmen Marañón, she told me that indeed she had, that Carmen was the premier hostess of Madrid! Through Robin Duke I got in touch with her, and along with Jane McBain we were asked to a party the following day. Going to the party was like going to the most fashionable gathering in the country. This was still the Franco era, but one was not particularly aware of politics, at least in our short stay. I remember well the ambience of the party (it could have been in New York, Washington or London), the head of the Prado there among others, no doubt the cream of the intellectual and social elite of Madrid. Carmen was welcoming. The apartment was magnificent: shelves of rare books and manuscripts, beautiful antique furniture and rugs, silver church reliquaries and an El Greco in the library! Delightful and so unexpected, but alas I lost touch with her again.

When the time came for me to go back to REAL LIFE in my hometown, Cambridge, I wrote a piece for the *Washington Post* entitled "On Leaving Washington:"

> What a variety of emotions we Washington transients feel as we leave this delectable city. First of all, one remembers the beauty of it: the sweep of Massachusetts Avenue as it

rushes down past the British Embassy; the symmetry of the reflecting pool with small figures sitting at its edge like a Seurat landscape; the Washington Monument stark white against a steely gray stormy sky; a sunny afternoon in September, the air full of the motes of autumn, walking along the C&O canal; the boats and canoes on the Potomac, like an eighteenth-century genre painting; or the loveliness of the White House which should be the cliché of all time, but never is.

One recalls the taxi drive from the National Airport along the grassy green parkway and across Memorial Bridge down into Rock Creek Park and up again into the leafy delights of Georgetown. One regrets all those trips to the zoo not taken; those postponed expeditions to Mount Vernon and the Lee Mansion; the dashes to the National Gallery, so seldom accomplished; those Senate hearings, so heedlessly unattended. And who will ever forget spring in Washington with its extravagant blooms, which I am sure is unmatched in any other city in the world, much less any national capital.

But I suppose the chief thing that strikes one on going home is that no matter what the administration, or what its politics, the talk is much better in Washington. I suppose by talk, I mean the bottomless cornucopia of rumors, half-truths, hearsay, name drops and tidings, good and bad, which is the daily fare of Washingtonians. No wonder other cities have not been able to develop gossip columns to compare with those of the nation's capital. The outlanders just don't have the stockpile of raw material. Their talk is therefore narrow-based and alas apt to be small-bore. They command the facts, statistics, know-how, special bits and pieces of knowledge, all admirable, but death to gossip. What do they know of the untrammeled speculation and the trial balloon, which those who have lived in the purlieus of power have learned to expect and to love?

Anyway, back in the provinces, we miss every minute of it. Wistfully we subscribe to the *Washington Post*, hoping to keep our hand in. But we know in our hearts that it's not the same as getting it fresh, dished up hot and piping over our morning coffee. Marshall McLuhan notwithstanding, the medium is not the message. You have to be there and sniff the air itself! And so all those who have been hooked on Washington will never feel complete until they are gathered once more to her seductive bosom.

On rereading this piece some decades later I thought that were I writing this today I might have struck a different note. Of course, everyone has their special memory of that wonderful city, and I fear that since my day it is a different place. So I shall remember it as I have written about it, the essence for me.

9

More Politics

ONE DAY IN THE SPRING OF 1968, I got a call from Bobby Kennedy asking me to go to Indiana to campaign "among the women" for his primary election. Somehow, I thought I had left politics behind when I moved back to Cambridge from Washington in 1967, but who could resist the fun of a campaign? It was a request that I could not refuse. Having gotten someone to take care of my dog, I soon found myself on a plane to Indianapolis, wondering where I could possibly fit in with the Kennedy women's famous coffee hours and receptions, an area where I felt sure they needed no help from me. As so often happens, in my first foray into the campaign headquarters, no one had ever heard of me, couldn't have cared less, and had no idea what to do with me. The gung-ho young coordinator of the so-called Speakers Bureau took one look at me with glazed eyes when I introduced myself and then looked away. There was going to be no help in that department. I could see myself falling between the cracks never to be heard of again. The situation was not only ridiculous, but also embarrassing. But knowing that initiative and gall are the essential ingredients of politicking, I began to look around to see where I might fit in.

I soon ran into Fran Martin, the wife of John Bartlow Martin, who had been Jack Kennedy's Ambassador to the Dominican Republic (and previously a Stevenson speechwriter). While her husband, a native Hoosier, was advising Bobby Kennedy how to campaign among his fellow Indianians, his wife had been tapped like me to work with "the women." In the eyes of the campaign strategists, "the women" were apparently an undifferentiated and indigestible lump, which had to be wooed and brought along by the aforementioned tea parties and coffee hours. Fran and I decided that that was not for us.

Taking matters into our own hands, we set off for Bloomington and Indiana University to win "the hearts and minds" of the faculty and students for Kennedy. Since the hearts and minds of the faculty and students had been pretty well won by Eugene McCarthy, the hero of the moment for his spectacular moral victory in the New Hampshire primary, we felt a bit as though we were entering an enemy camp. We stepped warily forth to begin our sorties, knowing that there was a certain amount of hostility towards Kennedy as a "spoilsport" for his late entry into the presidential race.

The haphazardness of politics always astounds me. I knew some people who knew some people among the politically active faculty wives, and in short order we were addressing evening meetings, making radio appearances, and downing the usual gallons of coffee as we spread the word. I think we had an impact, putting forth arguments in favor of Kennedy with such enthusiasm and hyperbole that, in comparing notes after one presentation, Fran and I realized that we had not only settled the Vietnam War on Bobby's behalf, but also recognized Red China in the bargain!

We wound up our personal campaigning in Indianapolis. At one meeting, I had the pleasure of running across one of those erstwhile young, macho Harvard Law School students who had given us such a pain in the neck trying to take over the Stevenson headquarters in Harvard Square a decade and a half before. Now, a somber and successful lawyer, he was all respect and attention to our speaking. I doubt whether he ever recognized me as that "irritating woman" who had once told him to "get lost."

Election night on May 7 was a triumph. The candidate's suite was jammed with workers, relatives, and newsmen milling about. Two or three TVs were blaring out the news, and the telephones rang incessantly. The noise was earsplitting. The atmosphere of excitement and high spirits was electric. Even Teddy White, author of *The Making of the President* series of books, left off observing the scene long enough to come and give me a kiss for old time's sake. My brother-in-law, John Fairbank, had been his tutor when he was an undergraduate at Harvard, and Teddy had been one of his favorite students.

I remember that Bobby was trailed wherever he went by campaign managers and the rest of the faithful (in campaigns, the one who sticks closest to "the body" apparently considers himself on the inside, inside track, and the candidate isn't even safe in the bathroom). Even so, he broke away at one point to come and thank Fran and me personally. He did it in the charming, oblique, and diffident way that was so characteristic of him.

As I wrote to my sister, describing the ins and outs of campaigning:

> Whether we deserved it or not, we had made a reputation for ourselves and no sooner had I returned to Cambridge than I received a call to rejoin the campaign in Oregon and California. But Oregon was a different kettle of fish! The Oregonians were like the Missourians; they had to be shown. And it seemed to me that Kennedy made a mistake running a campaign more appropriate to the conservatism and provincialism of Indiana than to the independence, political sophistication, and rather eccentric character of the Oregon natives. Most of them had already made up their minds for Eugene McCarthy, and the somewhat patronizing tone adopted by Kennedy and his cohorts didn't go down so well. In the end, as you know, he lost Oregon. However, it was fun to try to win the Oregonians over; their skepticism was so strong and their eccentricities so patent! The women were especially tough nuts to crack. It made me reflect that a lot of pioneer women had followed the Oregon Trail west, powerful figures who had left their mark unto the third and fourth generation. A matriarchal society if ever I saw one!

> I recall one of our democratic women mentors reporting during a drive to Eugene her strong conviction that "at night, when you're asleep, your washing machine and dryer are downstairs plotting with each other which one was going to break down tomorrow." And she wasn't joking. At one of our meetings in somebody's rec room, complete with black plastic banquettes and bunches of plastic roses, a woman suggested that there should be "group therapy" for the poor so as to get them back on the tax rolls. I thought it an interesting new angle, bizarre to say the least. This

didn't seem to have much to do with Kennedy's candidacy, but it was weird occurrences like these that one learned to take in stride.

It's the unexpected, the paradoxical, and the infinite variety of people and experiences which gives such zest to campaigning. Life is so out of sync with one's normal existence. For example, I found myself sitting in a dark gloomy bar at eleven o'clock the other morning, the smell of stale beer still permeating the air, or digging into a late lunch at 3:30 in the afternoon and overhearing negotiations between two smooth lumber merchants striking a deal at the next table. Not your usual day as a "housewife," though I mustn't overlook the fact that there are plenty of "housewives" out there striking a deal for themselves.

Each morning we members of his staff and campaign workers waved the candidate off from the steps of Portland's Benson Hotel, site of the Kennedy headquarters. Bobby would sit on the lowered hood of the open convertible, exposed in the most careless way, and acknowledge our send off with his usual kidding asides. I remember it so well, for it seemed so casual and so dangerous.

We used to run across the McCarthy campaigners from time to time. They were generally earnest, self-righteous, humorless young people, with regimental ties and neat clothes and the wackiest politics in the world. Among them was an anthropologist, I've forgotten his name, the type you and I have been trying to escape all our lives, like those dread graduate students who used to come to tea on Sunday afternoons at home and eat up all the good sandwiches before you could get a bite. This one, so hostile, demanding and sarcastic. The sort that has lately discovered politics as an outlet for his bristling ego!

But there were others, some you and I had known in other

incarnations and other settings who rather preferred the bar at the Benson where we were housed to the more mundane bar in their less chic headquarters down the street. It was strange to see the tall, rather drunken figure of Robert Lowell, the poet-in-residence to the McCarthy campaign, looming through the cigarette smoke with the deafening roar of talk and late-night revelry swirling around him. I had last seen him lunching with the English critic I.A. Richards at Chez Dreyfus in Harvard Square, no doubt involved in some esoteric discussion of modern poetry.

What a bizarre episode. There is something so fleeting and unreal about political campaigning. The people one meets along the way with whom one has instant rapport and who often pour out their innermost thoughts and are gone. No one remembers their names or yours.

My letter to my sister continued:

So we went on to California. What a lark! Whistle-stopping on the candidate's train through the Central Valley was the high point of the California campaign, as far as I was concerned. Of course, I had been on a campaign train once before when Stevenson was running, but this was different. The atmosphere was so buoyant and optimistic. The crowds, mostly Chicano field laborers, were ecstatic and the candidate at his best, joking and serious by turns, larding his speeches with slightly stumbled-over Spanish phrases. Someone had supplied the train with a crate of Bing cherries which we ate by the handful in between jumping off and on the train at each stop. I can still taste their juicy sweetness as I remember that extraordinary journey.

I hope you don't mind my using this letter as a kind of journal to remind me in my old age!

But to go on. At one point, as the staff and the newspaper-men milled around the tracks and cinder bed at the back of the train, while Bobby was addressing the usual huge throng from the rear platform of the train, a reporter from the *London Telegraph* approached to interview me as a typi-cal California housewife, I presume, concerning my opinion of the candidate. What a blow to my pride! I was so pleased with myself to be one of Bobby's campaigners. But I guess though I was out of sync with my usual daily habits, I must have kept something of the air of a domestic drudge! Does it show that much? Anyway, I had the pleasure of putting the English journalist rather tartly to rights.

The Monday before the primary election I was running to catch a ride to Palo Alto to keep a speaking engagement when I twisted my ankle stepping off a curb outside the Fairmont Hotel in San Francisco and broke a bone in my foot. It seemed sort of foolish to stay around and watch the results in Los Angeles with my aching foot, exciting as it would be. So I took a noon plane back to Boston. Otherwise I guess I would have been in the Ambassador Hotel when Bobby was shot. I have always been grateful that I was not.

Apropos of the speech that day, an amusing thing happened many years later when some candidate for Congress from our district came for a political meeting in my living room in Cambridge. His appointments secretary, a young Californian, drew me aside and whispered that she had told her parents that she was coming to my house and that they had recalled that I had spoken at a rally for Kennedy so many years ago at their house in Palo Alto. I was flattered to be remembered but in truth my only memories of the occasion were a feeling that my speech was a flop, that my foot ached, and someone came up afterwards

and said, "You'd make a great debater." I could hardly believe my
ears after what I thought was such a lousy performance. And so
the circularity of life repeats itself!

In October of 1968, I happened to be in Athens on my way
to Tehran to meet my daughter Christina, who was flying in
from Japan, where she had been traveling with her father after
her Radcliffe graduation. When the stunning news of Jackie's
impending marriage to Onassis was announced, Tom Winship,
editor of the *Boston Globe*, cabled me to write a story. With the
help of my cousin, a scholar of Greek mythology whom I was
visiting, I was able to get my classical allusions correct and
obliged with the following effort, quoted in part:

Saturday, October 19, 1968

ATHENS—The 24 daily papers of Athens, which have
been struggling under strict censorship for months, are at
last having a field day. The news of the forthcoming marriage of Jackie Kennedy and Aristotle Onassis was splashed
all over every front page on Friday with enormous photographs of all participants.

The story spilled over into three or four full-page spreads
and banished the Olympics and the flight of the Apollo
7 to the back pages. The fascinated though incredulous
Athenians mobbed the hundreds of newspaper kiosks all
over the city and snapped up the latest editions.

The Greeks identify the terrible tragedies of the Kennedy
family with the Greek myths, especially the myth of Atreus,
with its bloody violence and the murders of Agamemnon
and Orestes. Now the legend seems to be continuing
though in a different vein. The beautiful and tragic Jackie,

whom the Greeks have always adored, is about to enter another mythic chapter. Her Onassis, too, has become a fabled figure in his lifetime. He is the poor boy from Smyrna who began as a bellhop and who made an enormous fortune in shipping and other myriad pursuits. And now he was about to carry off the world's most legendary woman.

Strangely enough, Onassis is not considered a true Greek by his countrymen. He belongs to the international set, his ships are registered under foreign flags, and he seems on the whole indifferent to the welfare of his native land.

Although his fellow Greeks admire any man who can acquire such a large slice of the world's goods, they say of him, "He is not one of us." A King Midas figure in the modern world, he inhabits a kingdom of incredible wealth, largely untapped by any state, and wields the power that accompanies such riches.

But all Greeks love a wedding and the hysteria and excitement here grows. The hippies, most of them Americans, have taken to the caves of Crete, and Jackie to her jewel of an island. And once again Greece has exercised her ageless allure.

The only sour note to which I was privy was pronounced by a rather haughty and aristocratic Greek woman, a friend of my cousin and a partisan of Maria Callas, Onassis's spurned mistress. "How could anyone marry someone with those schoolgirl legs!" she remarked.

— 10 —

Return to Cambridge

OUR LIVES HAD CHANGED through the years. In 1970, Arthur and I were divorced. His new life included a new wife and a new job, professor of history at the Graduate Center of the City University of New York. I returned to the grand old Cambridge house where we had lived as a family for so long. After seven years of glitzy, unreal Washington and after thirty years of marriage, I felt depressed and disoriented. What to do with the rest of my life? It seemed to loom ahead for decades, empty and desolate. I had been an artist all my life, but even painting and drawing did not seem to revive my flagging spirits.

No doubt, I had changed during the hectic and tumultuous years in Washington, but perhaps Cambridge had changed even more. The sixties had arrived with a vengeance. It was easy in the old days to identify the absent-minded professor in black cape or flowing beard, which could only bespeak the academic eccentric here considered a local adornment and confirmation of the spaciousness of Cambridge tolerance. The tolerance remained, but the academic oddity had been lost in the forest of beards that had taken over the Harvard Yard.

Although Radcliffe graduates had been allowed to use Widener Library in my day, the girls were segregated in a small cell in the library's upper reaches where they could retire with their books. That was a millenium ago, and now the girls lived in the Harvard houses and the boys in the Radcliffe dormitories, and both were present in the stacks. With the usual perversity of the young, many students considered living in dormitories to be square and had fanned out into pads and apartments toward Central Square, Cambridgeport, and even into the former "no-man's-land" of Somerville. Young people found Cambridge a lively place and were willing to pay exorbitant prices to live in groups of four and five or more in comparative squalor. They had taken over whole chunks of housing formerly occupied by low-income families. They had displaced the natives and put the stamp of their lifestyle inexorably on the city.

Corner grocery stores, virtual neighborhood institutions, were replaced by health food marts selling macrobiotic nutriment. Local package stores, transformed into sophisticated wine and liquor emporiums, were presided over by recent PhDs in history and literature, who found the good life behind the counter, talking knowingly about the best year for Bordeaux, surrounded by fine cheeses and pâté, pickles in barrels, and French bread flown in from Paris. Ethnic restaurants flourished with people no longer nourishing themselves solely on bean sprouts and groats. Italian and Greek restaurants had been "discovered"; Mexican and Japanese restaurants had sprung into existence; and saloons, where local denizens had been embalming themselves since time immemorial, were suddenly upgraded to pubs with flickering gas lamps and Irish reels and ballads performed in the name of native culture.

Every Monday, an array of boys and girls often attended by large dogs, deployed themselves across the city, selling the *Boston Phoenix* and the *Real Paper.* They stood at street corners and stoplights, each seeming hairier and more spaced out than the next, though committed and zealous in their salesmanship.

And they were zealous, too, in their commitment to doing good works. A flower child of the period in tie-dyed skirt and Guatemalan *huipil* once rang my doorbell at six in the morning. When I finally stumbled down stairs to answer her ring, she stood there with tears in her eyes, holding a little box with a sick baby skunk inside, which she piteously begged me to cure. When I suggested that perhaps it would be sensible to put the little creature into the next world by artificial means, she objected gently but firmly, "Animals know how to die, just like humans." I presume she was "into Death," the latest fad. At last the pretty baby did expire, but not before the flower child had gone on her way, having done her good deed for the day, and leaving me to clean up the mess!

The effect of the youth invasion was catastrophic for many old people living on small retirement pensions or Social Security. Their cheap housing was being converted into co-ops and condominiums, and they were being driven out of Cambridge. A comparison of the death notices in the *Cambridge Chronicle* told the story. Some decades ago they might have read: Mrs.

Fanfani, born in Sicily, was brought to Cambridge as an infant and lived in Cambridge "all her life." Now, reports more often revealed that Mrs. McCarthy, "having lived in Cambridge until a few years ago," had moved to Everett or Lynn or back to Nova Scotia, where she was born, driven out by the high rents. People used to be "survived" by "offspring" of "the same address" or at least some other Cambridge address. Now, they died in distant places, and children were scattered to the four winds. It underlined how much the city had changed and how quickly the atmosphere these citizens brought to the community had evaporated.

Even my neighborhood, which had always seemed staid and unchanging—an academic redoubt if ever there was one—had not stood still. The ebb and flow of life seemed to have quickened. Middle-aged neighbors, once vigorous and active, had grown old and tottered down the street, if they tottered at all, on the arm of some hireling student.

In the late fifties our neighborhood was rather a gray one, occupied by virtuous, high-minded academics and the like, eating simple meals, watching just a touch of television—black and white, naturally—nothing, of course, that would disturb or corrupt the even tenor of our ways. But then something wonderful and amazing happened. Into the neighborhood and over the TV waves emerged Julia Child.

While we were in Washington in the 1960s, Julia Child and her husband, Paul, had moved to Cambridge, buying the house at 103 Irving Street. Our mutual friend Avis DeVoto, with her resolute perseverance and publishing know-how, had helped Julia get her first cookbook published. *Mastering the Art of French*

Cooking was offered originally to Houghton Mifflin, which, in its wisdom, after excruciating years of dilly dallying, turned it down. The book was afterwards offered and accepted by Knopf (lucky Knopf!).

And so in her charming way Julia Child led us into a new world of French cooking, quiches, crepes, *crème caramel, boeuf bourguignon*, and so forth and so on. Over the ensuing decades, of course, she changed the eating and cooking habits of the country in the nicest way, making it seem so easy and so possible. She was always the same kind, humorous, natural person as a TV personality as she was in real life. And did she ever put Irving Street on the map! Once when charging something at a store and giving my address on Irving Street, the clerk looked at me and spoke with baited breath, "You must be a neighbor of JULIA CHILD!" And I can report that accompanying Julia Child in public was like being present at a royal progress.

Ken and Kitty Galbraith had returned from India to their elegant brick house over the back wall, wispy Kitty who, despite her anorexic appearance, must have had a spine of steel not to have been squashed by the colossus beside her. Through the years the Galbraiths had been the soul of hospitality, giving an annual party in their backyard after commencement. It always involved the great and the near-great who might be visiting Cambridge either to receive an honorary degree or just to be present. As a matter of fact, we originally held the post-commencement party in our backyard before we went to Washington.

Irving Street once seemed to be peopled only by philosophers or professors of Sanskrit while sober members of the Divinity

School inhabited Francis Avenue. But that was a millennium ago. Academia had prevailed for two or three generations, but things began to "thin out" in the last three or four decades of the century. Even the Divinity School where generations of Unitarian and other Protestant divines were trained was changing, becoming the preferred spot for those finding themselves in mid-life crisis to spend a year or two deciding what to do next. Few went into the ministry.

A generation of graduate students who once hurried past my back door with their green baize book bags to bury themselves in laboratories and libraries had moved on, their places taken by succeeding generations with bulging knapsacks and babies in carrying contraptions to be deposited in the local day-care center. The neighborhood was dog heaven, with cars screaming down the streets in the early morning pursued by two or three large dogs being exercised before their masters went to the office. If the dogs weren't out, the driving schools were, with the tense faces of the tyros in sharp contrast to the visages of their instructors who looked as though they had had a hard night out on the town.

One year, the sound of the footfalls in early morning, heard through the open window, signaled the onset of the joggers, like the lockstep of a conquering army. At night, all was silence save for the whine of a burglar alarm, unanswered and unheeded, or the midnight squeal of brakes and the smell of burning rubber, as some hot-rodder hurtled through our deserted streets. However, all this mayhem never discouraged a devoted practitioner from performing tai chi on a nearby knoll as the sun was rising.

The presence of the Center for the Study of World Religions meant that it was not unusual to see a Tibetan lama or a Greek Orthodox priest out for a stroll. In fact, the Greek Orthodox priest was one of the early morning joggers, dressed in full black habit with beard flying, making no concessions to sweat suits or sportif dress except for a pair of psychedelic Adidas on his feet to save his arches.

Things had livened up somewhat since I had been away. Our good Rabbi Zigmond had retired, and under the aegis of the new head of the Hillel House the Jewish students in the spring on Bryant Street danced the hora and carried the Torah around in their arms with their prayer shawls over their shoulders and their yarmulkes on their heads, singing songs and brightening the atmosphere of this stronghold of Protestant austerity

Daniel "Pat" Moynihan and his family had moved into a house on Francis Avenue when he took up his teaching at Harvard. One might often see him wandering down the street with his little white dog for company, his diminutive tweed hat cocked over one eye, his "embonpoint" bursting out of his sheepskin coat, and a look on his rosy, beatific face that somehow told one that he was dreaming of other scenes and other fates. When President Nixon appointed him ambassador to India, Francis Avenue was dubbed "The Passage to India," serving both Galbraith and Moynihan as a byway to New Delhi!

The "Chuck" Dalys had moved into the house across the street, adding much to the fun and games of the neighborhood. In March, when our spirits were lowest and the long winter most unbearable, the Dalys threw their annual St. Patrick's Day Party.

"Chuck," who was in charge of community relations for Harvard, must have construed his job along quite different lines from his predecessors, believing that frequenting the Abbey Lounge in Inman Square and drinking with the regulars was as good a way as any other to soothe the neighborhood. He would import a trio of old boys from the Abbeyfeale to sing Irish songs and ballads to entertain his old pals, "Tip" O'Neill, Kenny O'Donnell, and Jimmy Breslin, among others. Even the president of Harvard on one occasion was seen to have attended.

At one of these galas, Nixon's sidekick, John Ehrlichman, was observed in the back seat of a monumental limousine parked in the street obdurately refusing to come in and join the gang. The motor was kept running for at least an hour for who knows what getaway? And who knows what he was doing within shouting distance of all those Democrats?

The festivities would continue far into the night. I would go home early since I was not the beer-drinking type. But even with my windows closed, the whoops and hollers and singing of Irish ballads, together with the flashing lights of the police cars drawn up on the curb, would wake me up in the early morning. The police weren't there to stop the mayhem. They had joined the party. For the old neighborhood of the philosopher William James, this was quite a switch. Though I suppose the observation of St. Patrick's Day is in a sense a religious celebration, I am not sure that Professor James would have considered this celebration a "variety of religious experience."

By this time, Ken Galbraith, along with Julia Child, had become something of an institution. TV trucks and cables often festooned Francis Avenue whenever any political (or otherwise) crisis arose when Ken was called upon to pronounce judgment thereon. Often if one walked around the corner there were stretch limousines parked in front of the house while some distinguished visitor came to sit at the great man's feet and receive his wisdom.

It must be said that Ken was not without ego. I remember on one occasion, Ken and George Ball, his old pal from the U.S. Strategic Bombing Survey (their report questioned the effectiveness of aerial bombing during World War II, enraging many in the military), going at it hammer and tong as to who had lately traveled the farthest and on the most significant assignment and, of course, had flown on nothing less than SSTs! I also remember going to dinner there and having a bet with a friend that two minutes wouldn't pass before Ken brought the conversation back "to him and his exploits." I won! At some point I had second thoughts—perhaps because Ken was slightly deaf he felt that as a gracious host he should keep the conversation going.

The visitors to Francis Avenue were sometimes of an exotic character. I remember that Benazir Bhutto, the beauteous Pakistani politician, a Radcliffe graduate and a Galbraith friend, came to stay with them when she received an honorary degree from Harvard in 1989. She was accompanied by an array of bearded, alarming-looking body guards, one a major general with clanking medals and gold braid epaulets, who were billeted across the street in the house of Mrs. Lord, a wonderfully nononsense elderly retired professor of Latin. No frills there! What a marvelous juxtaposition. Only in Cambridge.

The varied mix of people in the old neighborhood would, I am sure, have interested William James, who was apparently fascinated by personality, and possibly intrigued his brother Henry even more. When one recalls how boring Henry James thought Cambridge in his youth, the great novelist might have found it an edifying experience, under its new dispensation: plenty of strong-minded women to anatomize, from female art historians, psychoanalysts, and law professors, to political activists and poets. But, alas, not a grande dame in the lot!

Even Savenor's, the local market on Kirkland Street, was full of airs and swagger, under the patronage of Julia Child becoming more gourmet by the minute. The euphoria was spilling over in the case of John Savenor, the butcher, who insisted, on my return, much to my embarrassment, "You've got to kiss your butcher!" Old Mrs. Savenor, who had escaped a Lithuanian ghetto and mothered a tribe of purveyors, resembled some Sholom Aleichem character out of a past age. Enthroned behind the checkout counter like a cheerful Buddha, she fingered her old-fashioned cash register with the bravura of a concert pianist, her large and comfortable torso seemingly rooted to the spot.

Long a Cambridge institution, she was even more so now. She chewed on an onion bagel smeared with cream cheese, sipped her coffee, and talked on the telephone, while waiting on customers. She allowed few concessions to modern merchandising. Plain counters sufficed, and no endless belts sped the flow of groceries, making for fierce Saturday night pileups. Dog-eared paper bags were her solution to the filing system, two or three of them stuffed with receipts, bills, and the charges of the day.

Mrs. Savenor seemed to preside over an eccentric salon rather than the neighborhood market. From her chair behind the counter, she dispensed an endless flow of advice, old-world wisdom, sharp looks, admonitions, soft soap, and appropriate sighs, aspirated according to the political persuasion of the individual customer. A pretty Indian mother in sari and her well behaved black-eyed child would get a cheerful greeting from the guru behind the counter, while three bachelors, overstocked with smoked oysters and stuffed olives, would receive some no-nonsense advice on the staples they needed. There was a pat on the head for every child, "beautiful," no matter how scruffy, and a sigh of sympathy for some overwrought mother came seemingly straight from the heart. One might buy only a couple of cans of dog food or a loaf of bread, but after passing through the counter and being subjected to the ministrations of Mrs. Savenor, one felt cosseted and soothed. Or that was what was supposed to be felt!

Nothing escaped her eagle eye. Generations of young scoundrels had received her moral preachments for dipping into the bubble gum jar without benefit of pennies. Mrs. Savenor, who it must be said could sometimes be a bit light-handed herself, suffered in her turn the scrutiny of gimlet-eyed law school students unwilling to allow her the error of one red cent. The scene was a perpetual comedy. The whole family were all great performers with a highly developed sense of nuances in dealing with individual customers, especially people like Julia Child and the professional types who lived on the "right" side of Kirkland Street. One day I was amused to hear Mrs. Savenor yell the length of the store to Jack, the meat man, "Mrs. Galbraith wants her veal sent over right away," followed by the loudest of whispered aside, "Jackie's coming for dinner."

What to do with the rest of my life? That was the question. Slowly, slowly, I began to pull myself together, deciding to no longer bemoan the past but concentrate on the future. Then a fortunate opportunity came my way, which at last set my feet on a constructive path. My friend Esmee Brooks suggested I audit a remarkable course entitled "The American Landscape," given at Harvard by Prof. J. Brinckerhoff Jackson, an enormously witty, erudite, and gifted lecturer. Professor Jackson, who published an influential magazine called *Landscape,* described and analyzed in his lectures such phenomena as the evolution of the American farm, the historical importance of the porch in American culture, and the strip as a modern cultural manifestation. But it was his four or five lectures on the evolution of the New England nineteenth-century textile mill that particularly struck in me a resounding note.

I had spent almost every summer of my childhood on a farm outside Franklin, New Hampshire, a small mill town in the Pemigewassett Valley. Each year the family had trekked north through Lowell and Lawrence and along the Merrimack River where in Manchester, New Hampshire, the vast Amoskeag mills, once the largest textile mills in the world, stretched for miles along the water. With their smoke-blackened walls and the hum and clatter of machinery audible through the open car windows on a hot summer afternoon, these mills represented a significant milestone in the development of the industrial revolution in the

United States. I remember seeing the drab lines of workers, the men with black lunch boxes, the women in shabby coats with scarves over their heads, pouring out of the Amoskeag mills, across the bridges over the canals, as the late afternoon shifts ended. Though I had not been particularly aware of the architectural quality of the mill buildings, I recall once driving into the courtyard of one of them and being impressed by the huge scale of the cobble-stoned paved yard. There was something almost European about the space, like the enclosed piazza of Siena or a marketplace in some French town.

As a result of Jackson's lectures, I looked at these mills with new eyes. I began to see them with new appreciation, not only as industrial establishments, which by the 1970s were unfortunately in steep decline, but as stunning vernacular examples of nineteenth-century architecture. In my travels I had carried my paintbox in my baggage and had the good fortune to draw temples in China, Mogul palaces in India, baroque churches in Guatemala, and mosques in Morocco, along with more modest buildings in Ireland and Italy. So having been sensitized by Jackson's lectures, it seemed quite natural to take up my brush and pen and set out to make a record of some of these magnificent old mills. It was in many ways a labor of love to draw them before further decline turned them into utter ruins or before they were destroyed by the wrecker's ball.

And so I set forth on a sort of voyage of discovery, aboard my trusty Mustang, pencils and notebooks at the ready, and a vague map in my head of the Merrimack River valley. When I began in 1973, I drew the obvious buildings—the huge Amoskeag mills,

Mill in Pittsfield, New Hampshire *by MCS, 1973*
More images of the mills can be viewed in the Marian Cannon Schlesinger
Collection at the New Hampshire Historical Society website:
www.nhhistory.org/fromthecollection.html

constructed in high Victorian style with blood-red bricks and
large bell towers embellished with elaborate brickwork. There
was the dye-works building with its Italianate, flat-roofed bell
tower and fancy iron fencing and the elegant "finishing" building, made up of rusticated granite blocks. I had started my search
just in time, for both these great buildings were demolished in
short order in the name of urban planning, one of the more mis-
guided concepts dreamed up by city planners in the 1960s and
1970s.

Farther south on the Merrimack, in Lowell and Lawrence,
I parked my car in the seedy neighborhoods which surrounded these crumbling old behemoths and sat on any convenient

doorstep to do my drawings. Many years later, the federal government would recognize Lowell's fascinating heritage as one of the earliest sites of the industrial revolution in America by establishing parts of the city as a National Historical Park.

I also crisscrossed the state of New Hampshire like a presidential hopeful in an election year to do my sleuthing. I found it challenging and amusing to follow the course of small rivers which emptied into the Merrimack or the Connecticut rivers, taking back roads along little known streams, certain that I would find an old mill or the remains of one along the way. And so it happened on many occasions. For after all, if you were an entrepreneurial hustler in the nineteenth century, you could build a mill, no matter how small, to take advantage of the water power that existed in such abundance.

Spring and fall were the best times for searching. In summer the smallest mills were often hidden from sight by leafy trees, and winters were simply too cold even in my cozy Mustang. In the fall and spring when the chill became too great, I remember the relief I felt when spotting a Dunkin' Donuts and warming myself with a glazed doughnut and a steaming cup of coffee.

I learned to take notes rather than make finished drawings on the site, drawing sample windows with their granite lintels or detailing a portion of the iron grillwork or the fancy brickwork that often adorned the more exotic buildings. On the whole, I eschewed the use of the camera. By employing the artist's license I could strip off the plastic junk of so-called twentieth-century improvement, tear down disfiguring additions, replace ugly asphalt siding, and reveal the wooden clapboards or the brick walls

Mill in Durham, New Hampshire *by MCS, 1970*

beneath. With this information in hand, I would return to my studio and make the finished watercolors or wash drawings. Eventually I completed over eighty wash drawings or watercolors of such Italianate buildings as the handsome Boott Mills in Lowell as well as the Nashua mills, the many Claremont mills towering over the Sugar River, and the elegant eight-story granite mills in Newmarket.

The watercolors and drawings were exhibited at the Octagon House of the American Institute of Architects in Washington and at the Boston Museum of Science in 1976 during the bicentennial year.

One day, I fell into conversation with two cheerful old ladies who had dropped in to see the pictures. They both had worked in the Amoskeag mills, as had their fathers, who had emigrated from Scotland at the turn of the century. I had been brought up on the idea that "the satanic mills crushed the bodies and souls of the workers," so I was somewhat taken aback when, in response to my rather mournful questions about the hardships of mill work, they claimed, "We liked it. It got us out of the house. And all our girl friends were there." They obviously looked back on their employment as the greatest fun. So much for sociology!

It was for my own pleasure and in some degree from a sense of artistic responsibility that I made a record of these beautiful buildings before some inevitably fell into ruins. Perhaps, more important, the project was the best therapy I could have found to bring me out of my slough of despond and set me back on the path to the future.

Then I took another step. I rejoined a wonderfully Bostonian club, the Nucleus. It had been founded in 1921 by five Boston ladies, five creative spirits who thought it fun to present skits and plays for their own amusement and for the amusement of like-minded ladies who wished to join.

I had first belonged to the Nucleus in the 1950s, an interloper from Cambridge, which even in those days seemed to be a remote borough across the Charles River from Boston. I remember being scared stiff of the Boston ladies. They all seemed to be cousins or daughters or aunts or sisters-in-law, in and out of each other's houses on Beacon Hill or the Back Bay, or "places" on the North Shore or Dedham or other familial compounds. But once I took part in some skit or play and realized that these terrifying women were humorous and funny and willing to make fools of themselves, the atmosphere for me cleared somewhat. My final appearance before going to Washington in a skit as Mamie Eisenhower at last gave me confidence to feel one of the group.

Things had changed at the Nucleus in the ten years I had been absent. Cambridge was no longer an unknown quantity, and many new members, poets, artists, writers and above all, actors, had joined from across the river. The club met once a month from November to May when the season ended with a picnic in one of the beautiful "places" that some of our members inhabited.

One of the things that struck me forcibly on my return from Washington was the presence of old and rooted people, adding their lore and memories so important to enriching any community. Washington was a city of the ambitious young and avaricious middle-aged former office-holders turned lobbyists or lawyers, but there seemed to be no place for the elderly in the city's hierarchy. Perhaps they had all gone back to Oshkosh or Des Moines. But Boston and Cambridge were full of aging characters, and some of them were members of the Nucleus.

There was Phyllis Cox, the sister-in-law of Walter Lippmann, married to the portrait painter Gardner Cox and herself a gifted musician. With her shiny black ear trumpet in hand, she was a faithful attendant at concerts in Sanders Theatre as well as lectures and speeches in the New Lecture Hall, literary or political. She was a great mutterer and had no inhibitions in expressing herself in no uncertain terms. I once drove her to one of the annual Nucleus picnics. "Off with their heads" seemed to be the general theme of her remarks throughout the ride, whether it had to do with the driver of an oil truck who had the misfortune to be stopped at the same red light as we did and was told in a loud voice that his radio was TOO LOUD, or the owner of some ranch house, viewed as we drove by, criticized for its general color scheme—the wrong reds put side by side, a fireplug red house with fuchsia rhododendrons and magenta azaleas in front. And she herself in a crimson-colored get-up that looked like an ancient bathrobe and bright, rather dirty, cerise slacks.

I'll never forget her leaving her rather tatty "bathrobe" in my car, which I finally got back to her after she bombarded me with telephone calls demanding its return. One might have thought that I had misplaced her sables! I remember what a ravishing beauty she was as a young person, and now still full of spirits (and vinegar), rather a withered wreck, her hair thinning on top, dyed jet black with the white roots inevitably showing. But she was such an original and generous patron of so many causes all her life. And she was only one of many colorful characters that were numbered among our members.

Such was the feel of those years and the inevitable changes that occur in any lifetime. And above all hovered the hateful shadow of the Vietnam War.

—11—

Return to India

HAVING HAD A TASTE OF INDIA on my trip around the world in 1962, I was determined to return. Ten years later, invited to visit friends in New Delhi, I gladly accepted. For an artist and a human being, it proved to be a rare experience, never to be repeated.

As a child, I had always looked forward to our Saturday morning expeditions to the Boston Museum of Fine Arts. I remember poking around the rather musty and deserted corridors and exhibitions, discovering Egyptian scarabs and sarcophagi, Greek intaglios, and above all the Indian miniatures, of which there was a remarkable collection. I remember examining the tiny details of the brilliantly colored costumes and the fanciful architecture, the foliage of trees, the exquisitely painted animals, birds, and flowers. The legends beside the miniatures identifying their sources, as in "Mughal 16th Century," registered only vaguely, and names like Kota, Bundi, and Datia were completely meaningless. It was only when I returned to India in 1972 that these long forgotten names came suddenly into focus.

My travels in India in 1972 took place under remarkable circumstances. There still existed in those days that remnant of Empire "The Bogie Trip," touring by private railway car across the vast, astonishingly varied country. On first hearing the word, "bogie" sounded to me like a made-up, Anglo-Indian word out of Kipling, with faint overtones of old-school-tie archness. On further investigation, I discovered that it was a perfectly good English word meaning railway carriage. A bogie in its Indian incarnation was a parlor car with staterooms and a saloon, rich with mirrors and mahogany, gleaming with brass fittings, dark with heavy drapes, a monument to the influence of fustian Victorian interior decor, which seemed as a style to have lingered in India long past its day. In our country, the rail tycoons of the nineteenth century occupied just such dazzling vehicles as they traveled the Union Pacific and the Great Northern, surveying their domains. In the same manner, the Viceroys and high officials of the British Raj journeyed the length and breadth of India.

This kind of luxurious travel had long since disappeared in the United States. But in India it was a different story. The railway system was the lifeline of the country, and frustrated railway buffs found India the promised land. There was every example of steam locomotive still pounding the rails, coal and wood burning, brassbound and shiny or black and sooty. Steam whistles screamed through the night, and the consolidated timetable, thicker than a man's wrist, was the most fascinating reading since Kipling or the novels of John Masters.

We boarded our bogie one evening as it stood on a siding in the

Delhi station. It took us some time to find the car in the gloom, tripping over sleeping bodies on the station platform, hopping over hazardous tracks, climbing slippery stairs. But once inside the bogie, the drawing room, or saloon, appeared to have many of the attributes of an Oriental seraglio. On the floor lay mattresses covered with orange and magenta cloth and piled high with pillows wild with Gujerati embroidery and mirror work. A piece of shamiana material with a bursting sun design adorned one wall. Champagne in ice buckets stood on the ornate mahogany buffet next to a multi-branched candelabra ablaze with red candles.

This was to be the bar, the dining room, the gathering place, the all-round refuge of our land cruise, to which we returned each day after a hard stint of exploring and sightseeing. Since we were a party of eleven, rather more than the car usually held, it was also the dormitory for the overflow, quite the normal thing in India where most people slept on the floor, or, if lucky, on a mattress or bedroll. A cook and a bearer were in attendance, stowed away in the tiny passage at the end of the car. Using only a small charcoal stove, they produced a stream of delicious hot meals, scrambled eggs and bacon for breakfast, tandoori chicken for dinner, tea at all hours, and hot water in enormous brass pails for sponge baths.

At half past ten that first evening, a donkey engine came to fetch us and attach our bogie to the through-train going south. After a bewildering set of maneuvers, we were duly inserted into the body of the Frontier Express. The complications and planning involved in a bogie trip are immense: shifting a private car

Delhi, India *by MCS, 1972*

from one train to another, shunting it onto sidings, reattaching it
in the middle of the night to such romantically christened trains
as the East Bengal Mail or the Dehradun Express. No rail line
in the United States would tolerate it for a minute.

Our first stop was the capital of the princely state of Kota,
some three hundred miles south of Delhi. We had been "cruis-
ing" all morning through the lovely, green, irrigated countryside of eastern Rajasthan, unrolling like a Japanese scroll. The
Frontier Mail moved at a leisurely pace, providing time to observe the land and the people: enormous rivers so still and placid
as to resemble great sprawling lakes winding through unending
plains; hundreds of little whitewashed villages with peepul trees
and flower-bedecked Hindu shrines; and, from time to time,

strange, isolated hills breaking the distant line of the horizon, jagged with the spiky towers of brilliant white Jain temples.

Tourism in India, at least in the early 1970s, was practically non-existent outside the regular tourist runs. Hotel pickings were thin, cars hard to come by, and American Express checks as useful as scraps of paper. Travel in the backcountry was greatly enhanced if one had "connections." Our "connections" came up with three quite respectable cars and drivers at the Kota station, and we set off through the winding streets, over the Chambal River, to the medieval stronghold of Bundi, another former Rajput state, some thirty miles away.

The scene along our route was a constant delight. We passed herds of goats, wandering cows, snail-paced bullocks, men and women on bicycles and on foot, buses festooned with every shape and size of bundle, person, and transportable animal. The Rajisthani men wore huge turbans of a gorgeous pure orange hue, built out of sixteen yards of cloth. The men's clothes were always white. So were the oxen and the little villages and even the egrets picking their way through the irrigation ditches. The contrast with the blood reds, purples, and magentas of the women's saris was striking.

The countryside, were it not irrigated, would have been arid and desolate, like the mountains with their twisted trees and undergrowth. Kipling described this kind of landscape in *The Jungle Book* as "jungle." But having had a fixed idea in my mind that jungles were impenetrably lush with lanaes and exotic plants, breadfruit trees and orchids, dripping with snakes and flashing with birds of brilliant plumage, I had never understood his depiction until I came to central India. These jungles were scrubby and dry with stunted trees and tangled thorn bushes, cut by stony and inhospitable gullies. Man-eating tigers still prowled through them, descending from time to time on hapless villagers.

On the outskirts of town, in the quite hideous new palace of the Maharajah of Bundi, in a bar room realizing the dreams of a connoisseur of pure camp, there were the stuffed heads of four or five of these huge beasts. Hunting had been a favorite sport of the Maharajahs of Bundi, involving at one time hundreds of elephants, beaters, gun bearers, visiting princelings and British nabobs. The old fortified palace of Bundi, on the other hand, was pure enchantment. One came upon it without warning, as the road curved through the foothills and suddenly revealed a lake and walled town. The battlemented palace, ten stories high, crowned an ochre mountain, surrounded by chalky white houses. From a distance, Bundi was reminiscent of a southern Italian hill town, though the setting was harsher and there was a grandness of scale uniquely characteristic of Indian architecture. The architectural silhouettes and motifs were domes and bonnetted balconies. Roofed houses nestling at the base of the ramparts, the winding, teeming streets, the brilliance of the aquamarine sky, and the pervasive heat combined to produce a strong Mediterranean flavor.

One clambered up the narrow streets, peeping through doorways into inner courtyards, the outside walls of the houses often decorated with paintings of elephants, tigers, or richly bridled horses. Tiny, open-fronted shops lined the streets, elevated two or three feet above ground, with the usual jutting stone sill on which shopkeepers sat and transacted business. In the murky interior, craftsmen beat out copper pots, or planed wood, or pursued other family enterprises amid the general uproar of children, old people, dogs, and sacred cows. There were tinsmiths and dyers, fruit sellers and rice merchants, and a bewildering array of other purveyors. Silversmiths sold silver by weight, as was the ancient custom, and one could pick up heavy silver bangles of great antiquity for a song, which were relatively expensive in the Delhi antique market.

A cobbled ramp led up to the palace gateway in a series of switchbacks. One could imagine a royal procession of dazzling caparisoned elephants, with the Maharajah and his courtiers seated aloft in jeweled howdahs, or the court ladies in strict purdah borne in curtained palanquins on the shoulders of slaves and servitors. The heavy doors of the palace's main gate were studded with enormous iron spikes, designed to ward off enemy elephants used as battering rams. Although no longer lived in, the palace had a light, pleasant atmosphere, as if the occupants had not been long gone. No matter what hidden flight of stairs one climbed, it always led into some secluded courtyard or airy terrace, at once private yet accessible through a network of ramps and staircases that joined every level at four or five different points.

The Rajput builders of the sixteenth and seventeenth centuries had a highly sophisticated grasp of air conditioning. Around every courtyard was arranged a suite of rooms, dark and cool, each with windows decorated with intricately carved marble screens

Village in India *by MCS, 1972*

or with stone canopied balconies, calculated to catch even a breath of air. On every hand there were shady spots in which to escape the intolerable heat, the cross drafts often coming from four sides. On the various levels there had once been full gardens with leafy fruit trees, flowers, humming birds, and fountains. Water once flowed through marble troughs, cooling the air and delighting the ear with its murmur.

It was not until 1931 that Bundi for all practical purposes became accessible to the outside world, and it was still far off the beaten track and visited only by the most enterprising tourists. The city was famous in the sixteenth and seventeenth centuries as the site of a school of artists who produced some of the most beautiful Rajput miniatures, many of them in the Boston

Bengal Tiger by MCS, 2008

Museum of Fine Arts. On the palace walls were frescos of the same genre, the colors dominated by brilliant turquoise blues. Depictions of battles and royal processions, of horses and elephants, were well preserved, considering the exposure to the elements over hundreds of years.

On our return to the bogie from Bundi, we fell upon our pallets, reached for our cocktails, and, when sufficiently revived, began to plan our next foray. One of our party had brought along a history of Hindu architecture published in Calcutta at the turn of the century. On leafing through its moldy pages with their faded photographs, we discovered that fifteen miles from our next stop, Jhansi, was one of the jewels of Rajput architecture. If Bundi was like a dreamlike evocation of *The Arabian Nights*, our next discovery, Orchha, a deserted community of palaces and Hindu temples, was like some bit of magic summoned up by an obliging genie for our private delectation.

When we arrived in Jhansi, our drivers denied that there was anything at all to see in Orchha and tried to dissuade us. We waved them aside, secure in our superior knowledge, and set off across the gently rolling countryside. Eventually, coming over a slight rise, we saw far away, misty in the morning heat, a forest of towers and temple spires, like some faintly remembered illustration by Edmund Dulac for *Bluebeard* or *The Sleeping Beauty*. As we approached, the extraordinary number and variety of palaces and temples became apparent. Driving through a tiny hamlet of a dozen houses, we felt, as the discoverers of Angkor Wat must have felt, waves of excitement and incredulity.

The little village itself was a gem—freshly whitewashed houses with lacy door jams decorated with floral designs in bright greens and yellows, and the doors themselves painted a cobalt blue. Newly dyed saris and enormous turban lengths of garnet-red cloth hung on poles to dry. Although the villagers watched us curiously as we wandered through the streets followed by children and dogs, the quiet of the hamlet was striking. In front of each house was a broad stoop built of hardened mud, a foot or so above the street, serving a purpose rather like a front porch in an American Midwestern town. The business of life was carried on there. Women squatted, nursing infants or sewing or preparing food. Old men sunned themselves. Children jumped and played or whispered together in clumps under the watchful eyes of their elders. The stoops discouraged wandering cows from invading the living quarters and kept houses from being flooded in the monsoon. I was impressed once again how well adapted Indian domestic architecture was to the needs of the people: flat surfaces for sitting, of which there was a great deal, shady trees in the village square, and thick mud walls to ward off the intense heat.

The palaces towering over the village almost overwhelmed the tiny community. And they were utterly deserted! We crossed an ancient arched bridge and passed through huge, decaying, iron-spiked wooden doors in crenellated walls into a sort of compound. Three palaces, one above another, climbed to a stupendous height. Monkeys pranced lightly from balustrade to balustrade, sneering and smirking, giving us an eerie feeling that we had invaded their private domicile. The smell of bat dung was acrid and unpleasant as we climbed the endless staircases, marveling at the elegance and taste of the Rajput architects— their sense of site, their feeling for balance and harmony, their wonderful mastery of scale. They were the ultimate romantics!

Across this metropolis of palaces was a stupendous Hindu temple of blue-gray stone, piling up ten stories high, and beyond, more palaces, whitewashed and filigreed like wedding cakes. The walls encircling the palaces, built of the same beige sandstone, were in turn surrounded by a sluggish keep full of reeds and rank undergrowth. Beyond was a broad, slow-moving, many-channeled river, rocky and sedgy, with herons and cranes wading in the shallow water. In the distance, the true jungle, impenetrable and wild, stretched as far as the eye could see.

Below were the huge, empty marshaling yards and stone sheds

for herds of elephants and stables for hundreds of horses. Here again monkeys cavorted over the crumbling roofs, rooks and vultures preened their wings, and green parrots flew in and out of nests in crannies in the walls. Their cawing and chattering and the distant chugging of the machinery of the village's deep well were the only sounds. In the choked, wild gardens of the palaces, acres and acres of gardens, little temples with characteristic bonnet-shaped stone canopies stood as memorials on the sites where wives of the Maharajahs had committed suttee, flinging themselves on the funeral pyres of their husbands.

All this beauty was falling into ruins. It was a story repeated over and over again throughout India with its incomparable architectural heritage and its hopeless poverty. What other countries may have in the form of great churches or palaces or monuments in the hundreds, India has in uncounted thousands, and there are no doubt many more treasures such as Orchha in the backwaters of this extraordinary country.

A colonel in the Indian Army came aboard our bogie to have a drink when we stopped at Gwalior on our way back to Delhi. He had been stationed in Jhansi, and we asked him if he had ever been to Orchha. "Oh, yes," he said. "I used to jeep through it to hunt tigers in the jungle miles beyond. Great tiger country! But I don't remember Orchha especially. Just a little village we drove through."

Ah, for the seeing eye!

—12—

Things Change

I DISCOVERED, MUCH TO MY SURPRISE, that I could live alone quite happily in spite of the fact that most of my life had been spent surrounded by hoards of people, the extended family of my childhood and youth, a husband, four children, and a stream of guests coming and going. Yet it all took time. In the end, a sort of three-dimensionality evolved. Instead of being torn in a hundred different directions, I felt restored to myself.

Living alone perhaps rather exaggerated my situation. I made the third floor into an apartment and rented it to what seemed a virtuous divinity school graduate student who turned out to be something of a sadomasochist, beating up on his pseudo live-in girlfriend from time to time. At last the mayhem got so bad that I finally threw him out. A great candidate for the ministry, I thought! I have no idea how he got into the house in the first place, probably pawned off on me by some unkind friend. He was succeeded by a dear Quaker lady who had such wimpy boyfriends that I was tempted to protect her from her own good nature. She

Irving Street, Cambridge, Massachusetts, 2011

allowed them to impose on her so much. But I restrained myself.

Two of my renters were wooed and won on my top floor, the most spectacular being a pretty blonde who was viewed by her putative husband as she raised money for PBS during one of those spring TV marathon auctions. He fell head over heels in love and wooed her in a gold-hued Jaguar, thereby raising the standards in the neighborhood a few notches while it was parked in the backyard driveway.

Sally Fitzgerald, the editor of Flannery O'Connnor's book of letters, *The Habit of Being*, rented the little room at the top of the backstairs as an office for fifteen years. She lived down the street in a house filled with children and grandchildren. A very erudite woman, she was someone to whom I often turned to verify some classical allusion or historical fact. We also indulged in literary gossip or chat about our mutual friends.

Speaking of being "restored to myself," I am reminded of a trip I took to France with friends one spring when I first felt intimations of this return to "wholeness." We spent the night in Vézelay, planning to go to Mass the next day in the cathedral. I had gotten up early and wandered off to sketch the virtually empty gardens on the ramparts near where St. Bernard had sent forth the folk on the Second Crusade in 1145. I recall the utter stillness in the air and the beneficent mildness of the morning sun as I sat drawing the cathedral from the back. There were rooks in the trees cawing and muttering from time to time and hawks soaring over the lovely green cultivated fields stretching to the horizon. This had been a famous land for hawking and falconry in the old days and still followed in that tradition. I remember sitting on an old iron bench under the great plane trees, my paints beside me, a sketch book on my lap, a good sharp pencil in my hand, doing what I wanted it to do, and feeling a sense of profound well-being, as though I were wrapped in a cocoon of depthless comfort. It was but the mood of a very brief moment, but one which for some reason struck deep into my consciousness.

We went on to Mass in the cathedral. Such a delicious experience. The choir sang beautifully, accompanied by the organ, a recorder, brass horns and some kind of rattle. The "nouvelle vague" in the Catholic service had obviously come to France.

A little sparrow flew around the enormously tall apse and the Dominican priests in their simple white habits so reminiscent of Zurbarán's paintings of Dominican friars added to the luster of the plain, mellow, off-white of the stones of the Romanesque basilica. The Mass was sung in French, sounding perhaps more mellifluous than the Boston-accented services of our native land. Speaking of accents, I was delighted by the final note struck by a little boy passing the collection basket wearing a t-shirt emblazoned with "The University of Texas."

People seem to be deserting us left and right as in any community as varied as ours in which academics are being "called away" or career changes are taking place. Pat Moynihan's dream of "other places and roles," as I had imagined, had come to pass as he departed for Washington, D.C., to work for Nixon and was eventually sent by President Ford to represent the United States at the United Nations. Of course, he later became the distinguished Senator from New York. The Dalys moved away when Chuck was appointed to some prestigious post at the Kennedy Library, there to protect all things Kennedy. Even the Jewish students no longer danced the hora or sang songs on Bryant Street as the Hillel House moved to an elegant headquarters in the midst of the Harvard Houses. So, quiet and decorum descended once more.

By the early 1970s, the children had scattered to their various lives and jobs from Santa Fe to California, from Denver to New York. I had finished my mill drawings and my trusty Mustang had finally collapsed. When my foot at one point went through the rusted-out floor and the engine almost fell out of its housing, I decided that perhaps the time had come to say goodbye and sold it for $50 to an apple-cheeked youth, thrilled to have one of the "originals," who no doubt restored it to its pristine glory and sold it for a fortune.

One day I had a visit from the writer Jane O'Reilly whose grandmother had been a classmate of my mother at Radcliffe, class of 1899. Jane came to ask me what I thought were the qualities of these remarkable women that might have meaning for the emerging women's movement and help sort through the dilemmas and confusions of the 1970s. We agreed that these women partook of a kind of buoyancy, courage and intellectual vivacity, together with an optimistic zest for life and willingness to put themselves on the line for causes they believed in. Certainly my mother was not afraid of either new ideas or situations, unimpressed by power or place, and I am sure it never crossed her mind that she was inferior to any man. My mother had come blithely east to college from the "wilds" of Minnesota, and, as I remember, Jane's grandmother came from Kansas City. They were rather exotic figures among a group of girls primarily recruited from New England.

Jane O'Reilly had planned to write a book on the subject of these women, but I don't think she ever did. Our conversation caused me to reflect, and I began to think seriously about writing something myself.

I had three children's books under my belt, and I had written pieces for the *Washington Post* and a few book reviews for the *Boston Globe*. At one point after I came back from Washington, I wrote a long piece for the *Globe* on "How Cambridge Has Changed." At about the same time, my literary guru, Avis DeVoto, handed me a book, *Period Piece*, by the English writer Gwen Raverat, and said, "Marian, you must read this book!" Gwen Raverat was the granddaughter of Charles Darwin, and the book was a charming memoir of her childhood spent with Darwin, Huxley, and her Wedgewood uncles, aunts and cousins in the rarified academic atmosphere of Cambridge, England. The book gave me an idea. Why not write about my memories of my childhood spent in less rarified academic Cambridge, Massachusetts?

I had plenty of source material, primarily the ten volumes of family letters, carefully bound, written over the years from Cambridge by my mother to her mother in St. Paul, Minnesota. My mother was a demon letter writer and a witty one, and she wrote not only of the basic family doings but of the passing show, life in general and academic life in particular. These volumes had sat on my brother's shelves for years, a treasure trove of information about a period and a kind of academic, social and political Cambridge life which has long since disappeared. The volumes somehow represented a constant challenge and a subtle rebuke. Someone should DO something with them, but what and when and who?

What finally impelled me to take the plunge was a visit I made to my friends, Sheila and Myron Gilmore, in Italy. While we were away in Washington, Myron had been appointed director of the Harvard University Center for Italian Renaissance Studies at the Villa I Tatti in Florence, once the home of Bernard Berenson, the famed connoisseur of Italian art, who had deeded the villa, his priceless art collection, and his superb library to Harvard with an endowment to establish the center. So Myron and Sheila had gone off to live in the beautiful villa and oversee the ten or more post-graduate students who each year had the good fortune to be part of the exotic establishment.

During my visit I had the good luck to stay in the room high up in the villa said to have once been occupied by Edith Wharton. The room not only looked out on the lush gardens of the villa lined with magnificent dark cypresses and a stunning view of the Arno valley, but it also housed Berenson's wonderful collection of novels, essays, biographies, Edwardian memoirs, travel diaries, and collected letters—everything one would want to read from Evelyn Waugh to Freya Stark, from Virginia Woolf to Aldous Huxley, from E.M. Forster to Henry James. When I finally dragged myself away from such good company and such delectable food, so rich had been the intellectual diet that on my return to Cambridge I began to think seriously of writing.

I had already taken a few tentative steps of exploration, having given a talk on "Interesting and Original Cambridge Women" at the Cambridge Public Library and published an article in *McCall's* entitled, "A Paintbrush in My Baggage," describing a trip to Italy taken with my mother and three sisters when I was seventeen years old. Both became the basis for chapters in my book.

I began by slogging through the many pages of my mother's letters. Slogging is perhaps not the word to use as I so often came on amusing and witty passages, descriptions of her growing up in St. Paul at the end of the nineteenth century and her life as a Radcliffe student, her comments on the First World War while my father was in the army in France, her descriptions of my brother and three sisters and myself as children. The material was fascinating but as a researcher I was a raw tyro, misplacing notes, misquoting passages, forgetting where I had left whole chunks of the manuscript. Halfway through and feeling rather overwhelmed by the task I had set myself, I received a letter from Ned Bradford, the editor in chief of Little, Brown, saying that he had heard that I had "a book" and that he would be interested in looking at it and would I have lunch with him "at the Ritz" on such and such a date. What more could I ask? It was the stuff of dreams!

So we had a delightful lunch and in my usual habit I can remember what I had for lunch, a Ritz specialty, lobster salad. I had taken along two finished chapters and on the basis of them he sent me a contract, which I signed in fear and trembling, afraid I might never be able to "come through" with the manuscript. I think Ned Bradford wondered about it himself. But I finally delivered the finished product, my memoir of Cambridge, a light-hearted answer to Gwen Raverat's *Period Piece*, entitled *Snatched From Oblivion: A Cambridge Memoir*, which was published in the spring of 1979. To my misfortune, I suffered the loss of my kindly patron Ned Bradford, who died on the day of publication. I felt like an orphan!

The book must have struck some chord for though it had a modest sale in contemporary blockbuster terms (it still sells) it elicited a stream of letters from nostalgic Harvard "old grads," Cambridge High and Latin School classmates, China buffs, former law students recalling their three-year grind, academic types recognizing scenes from their world, and casual Cambridge visitors fascinated by the so-called ambience of the community. I even had a touching letter from a man who said that he had read it aloud to his dying wife.

It had the distinction of being read aloud in its entirety over WGBH, the local Boston Public Radio station. During one long hot June month, having broken my leg in a freak accident, I lay in bed and listened to my deathless prose coming over the air-waves every weekday evening, and later I ran into people who had heard snatches of the book read over their car radios as they were stuck in traffic on their nightly commute home.

Cambridge apparently goes through radical changes every few decades and of late seems to be growing ever more cosmopolitan and various. Pockets of Haitian immigrants have settled near Central Square where one often hears French and Creole spoken on the street. The Spanish-speaking population has grown so pervasive with the influx of Puerto Ricans, Mexicans, and other Latin Americans that many public notices are printed in Spanish as well as English. A vibrant Brazilian community, concentrated in Somerville, has spilled over to Cambridge. And the Asian influx, especially in the case of Harvard and MIT students, is remarkable.

At the other end of the city, the rich and the famous and the not so famous but rich anyway, are buying up the wonderful old Victorian mansions and other behemoths for millions of dollars and then spending millions more to "do them over," Cambridge has been discovered as a great city in which to "hide out," a wonderful city in which to sink into anonymity, if that is what you want, as most people are too preoccupied with their lives to pay much attention to their neighbors. The natives are not necessarily snobs, just busy!

I once complained to a friend that with all these solid citizens taking up residence the eccentrics and originals who seemed to have peopled my childhood would be overpowered. Her only response was, "Just because you are rich and famous doesn't mean you can't be weird!"

Across the street from our house on Irving Street, atop Shady Hill, now stands the headquarters of the American Academy of Arts and Sciences, replacing the lovely nineteenth-century mansion of Charles Eliot Norton (in the 1950s torn down by Harvard in its wisdom) where I attended chamber music concerts as a child. The park around the handsome modern building is colonized by a veritable army of dog owners exercising their pets. In the old days, as the children were growing up, we made friends through the PTA and other groups; now we make them through our dogs.

Harvard has grown into a colossus, bigger, richer and hungrier by the day. Its ravening appetite for building and expansion is so great that we neighbors have to keep our eyes open lest we be swallowed whole. To be sure, the university has had to alter its ways, especially in relation to the city of Cambridge. Smooth operators have taken the place of the arrogant, let-the-chips-fall-where-they-may types who used to dominate the town-gown scene when there was an undeclared war between City Hall and

Marian, her son Andrew and grandson Hugh at their Irving Street house, Cambridge, Massachusetts, 1992

the Harvard powers that be. The destruction of the Norton estate would never be allowed today with all of us preservationists getting into the act. We only hope that Harvard's knowledge and learning expand at the same rate as its real estate.

Of late, erstwhile monarchs, dictators, defeated politicians, intellectuals of every stripe, musicians and writers, world famous scientists and theologians, are made so welcome that the list in the *Harvard Gazette* of their available lectures, seminars, readings, and concerts is positively mind-boggling. The generosity of the old and new grads pouring their gold into the university's coffers is rewarded by their names being forever incised in granite in the new university buildings or attached to distin-guished professorships. And so their names go down through the ages.

In the meantime, we sit in our houses now worth millions of dollars that we paid a pittance for sixty years ago and realize that we are the last of a breed, academics and simple citizens living well beyond our desserts in old-fashioned academic enclaves about to go down the drain.

And so one goes on with one's life!

MCS's studio in Cambridge, Massachusetts, 2011